Assistive and Instructional Technology

PRO-ED Series on Autism Spectrum Disorders
Second Edition

Edited by Richard L. Simpson

Titles in the Series

PRO-ED Series on Autism Spectrum Disorders
Second Edition

Assistive and Instructional Technology

Kevin M. Ayres

Erinn Whiteside

pro·ed
An International Publisher

8700 Shoal Creek Boulevard
Austin, Texas 78757-6897
800/897-3202   Fax 800/397-7633
www.proedinc.com

© 2018 by PRO-ED, Inc.
8700 Shoal Creek Boulevard
Austin, Texas 78757-6897
800/897-3202   Fax 800/397-7633
www.proedinc.com

Library of Congress Cataloging-in-Publication Data

Names: Ayres, Kevin M., author. | Whiteside, Erinn, author.
Title: Assistive and instructional technology / Kevin M. Ayres, Erinn Whiteside.
Description: Second edition. | Austin, Texas : Pro-Ed, Inc., [2018] | Series:
  Pro-Ed series on autism spectrum disorders
Identifiers: LCCN 2017039886 (print) | LCCN 2017051053 (ebook)
  ISBN 9781416411499 (ebook)
  ISBN 9781416411482 (paperback)
Subjects: LCSH: Autistic children—Education. | Children with
  disabilities—Services for. | Educational technology. | Instructional
  systems. | Self-help devices for people with disabilities.
Classification: LCC LC4718 (ebook) | LCC LC4718 .A97 2018 (print)
| DDC
  371.33—dc23
LC record available at https://lccn.loc.gov/2017039886

Art Director: Jason Crosier
Designer: Lissa Hattersley
This book is designed in Nexus Serif TF and Formata Sans.

Printed in the United States of America

1 2 3 4 5 6 7 8 9 10   26 25 24 23 22 21 20 19 18 17

Contents

○│○ From the Editor

Children and youth with autism spectrum disorder (ASD) routinely demonstrate exceptionally demanding and distinctive characteristics and needs. Even when compared with other disabilities, ASD is especially complex and perplexing. Learners diagnosed with ASD exhibit a range of cognitive and communication abilities and social interests; they also commonly display a variety of challenging behaviors. Still, many children and adolescents with ASD have normal patterns of growth and development and a wide range of distinctive assets and capabilities, and some individuals with ASD have highly developed and inimitable abilities. These widely varied and unique features necessitate specially designed interventions and strategies orchestrated by knowledgeable and skilled professionals. When supported by the right combination of well-informed professionals (and, in many instances, parents and family members) and appropriate methods and intervention strategies, children and youth with ASD show significant progress. Without a doubt, consistent and correct use of effective methods, as presented in the current "how to" series, is the key to achieving successful outcomes with individuals with ASD.

Preface to the Series

Identification, correct implementation, and ongoing evaluation of scientifically supported and effective practices are essential features of effective programming for learners with ASD. Unquestionably, there is a clear-cut link between use of interventions and supports with empirical backing and positive school and post-school outcomes. Different terms, including *evidence-based procedures and practices*, *scientifically supported interventions*, and *research-validated methods*, all refer to methods and practices that have been successful in bringing about desired changes based on objective and empirically valid research Unfortunately, practitioners all too often fail to use these proven tools and procedures, or use them the wrong way.

Indeed, this "research-to-practice gap" is a major obstacle in efficiently and effectively addressing the needs of learners with ASD and creating optimal pathways to the best outcomes. This is not a problem of motivation, intent, or objective. Educators and other professionals, as well as parents, families, and other stakeholders, want the most effective methods and updated ASD information. Regrettably, clearly written and practitioner- and family-friendly materials that provide straightforward and user-friendly information and explanations are in short supply.

This concern was the motivation for creating the current resources. Each book in the series provides utilitarian and down-to-earth information on using an intervention or support method with potential to produce significant benefit. Each book, written in a user-friendly and straightforward fashion by experienced internationally recognized professionals, offers practical information, solutions, and strategies for successfully supporting individuals with ASD and related disabilities.

The 10 books in the series offer clear and direct guidance on applying research-supported and proven information, methods, and procedures. The series has the potential to make a significant positive difference for teachers and allied professionals.

Several of the books focus on using applied behavior analysis (ABA), the single most verified intervention tool for learners with ASD. The revised series includes the following:

- De Boer provides step-by-step use of discrete trial instruction and related methodology.
- Sturmey provides guidance on implementing ABA-based verbal behavior methodology.
- Tincani, Lorah, and Dowdy direct readers in how to design maximally effective management programs via functional behavior assessment and analysis.

Other skill development foci are covered in the series, each with an emphasis on practical application of documented methods, as evidenced in the following:

- Stichter and Conroy address the ever-pressing issue of building social skill assets among children and youth with ASD and harnessing the support of peers.
- Charlop provides a practitioner-friendly explanation of use of naturalistic teaching strategies and incidental teaching methods.
- Ayres and Whiteside provide essential and utilitarian information on how to take advantage of assistive and instructional-technology tools to teach and support learners with ASD.
- Earles-Vollrath, Cook, and Kemper, in detail, describe efficacious visual supports that can help children and youth with ASD function more effectively and independently.

- Crutchfield and Wood provide readers clear-cut instruction in the use of cognitive behavior modification, self-management, and self-monitoring methods.
- Shogren and Wehmeyer, via their book on self-determination, offer specific and clearly described strategies for ensuring that individuals with ASD are fully and deservedly involved in their program plans and outcomes.
- Finally, Travers addresses the all-too-often-neglected topic of sexuality matters among adolescents and young adults with autism-related disabilities.

Richard L. Simpson
Series Editor

1 Introduction

Technology, broadly speaking, encompasses every tangible thing in our environments, from pencils and chairs to computers and cell phones. In contemporary education and therapeutic contexts, technology usually refers to the "high-tech" (computer-based) end of this continuum that may assist with learning. This book is designed to give practitioners a step-by-step guide to using technology to enhance the learning of students with autism spectrum disorder (ASD). Drawing on the extensive research base for assistive and instructional technology, this book will help to explain various technologies and how they can be applied in the classroom or other learning contexts. The emphasis is more on the application of readily available tools that teachers can customize to meet the learning needs of their students rather than on packaged, purpose-built software. While the book covers commercially available models, the emphasis is on technology tools that teachers can use in creating their own instructional and assistive technology.

One of the challenges in writing a text about how to use any technology involves consideration for the life span of the text that is written. The evolution of technology will consistently outpace researchers' efforts to evaluate it (Ayres, Mechling, & Sansoti, 2013). Many tools and software packages will come to market before they are fully vetted. Therefore, this book aims to help practitioners identify key features to look for in new technology while giving them the step-by-step support they need to use that technology effectively. Likewise, the book emphasizes critical aspects for instruction that practitioners should include in the technology-based materials they create. Technology, like a textbook, is simply a tool that we can use to enhance educational progress. Failing to understand how to best implement technology-based solutions may disrupt the learning environment and slow educational progress. While the book discusses many of the advantages technology may have over nontech options, the underlying theme is that those practices that work with low-tech materials often work with high-tech materials. Considering technology as existing in a separate realm, as something special, has a tendency to cause people to ignore what they already know about evidence-based teaching methods.

This book does not promote the use of technology simply for the sake of using technology. Rather, this book emphasizes how and when to use technology to maximize student gains and increase the efficiency of instruction. While using the latest technology on the market has appeal and may motivate students, practitioners should find other tools to support instruction if the technology does not help address a student's needs. Technology provides a host of advantages. The technology may collect data, provide feedback, and free the teacher to work with other students. However, if it does not result in improved learning outcomes, practitioners must find other tools. McCleery (2015) suggested that harnessing the capabilities of technology to address the intricate needs of individuals with autism would require practitioners (e.g., behavior analysts, teachers, and speech pathologists) to work as codevelopers with industry. Until that occurs, practitioners can capitalize on many readily available tools to help meet their student or client needs; they must just proceed with an awareness of how to match the evidence base to the technology and the technology to their client's needs. This book will help practitioners learn to pinpoint critical aspects in current and emerging technologies that have a foundation in the research to support their use, and, once identified, to use those technologies in a manner consistent with current science.

Forecasting the next big innovation in technology is an industry unto itself. In terms of technology and education for individuals with ASD, most of the innovation has come from more analog types of practices (paper and pencil). Speech-generating devices (SGDs) were preceded by communication boards that relied on photographs or drawings. Video modeling on mobile devices followed the use of video modeling on videocassettes. Some commercially successful software packages descended directly from one-on-one instructional procedures manualized by Ivar Lovaas (cf. Lovaas, 2003). This historical context is relevant because as technology changes and as practitioners adapt procedures to capitalize on available technology, we have to attend to the underlying processes. Moreover, we have to recognize that evolution will be gradual, which will allow practitioners and researchers to help guide the advances by carefully evaluating practices and sharing outcomes. As this text focuses on technology uses, a special effort is made to maintain an emphasis on the basic learning mechanisms responsible for change and not to overshadow that with the novelty of (what is today) new technology. Getting too caught up in the latest contemporary trends will render this text obsolete; focusing on the learning process, though, should permit readers to adapt newer technologies based on their understanding of how to integrate technology in general into evidence-based practice. Kientz, Goodwin, Hayes, and Abowd (2013) categorized eight different technologies for individuals with autism, including robotics and virtual reality. Our discussion focuses on those technologies most frequently found in classrooms where there is sufficient evidence to advocate their use.

What Are Assistive Technology and Instructional Technology, and How Are They Related?

Before beginning a general discussion of using technology as a tool for teaching, we need to establish that technology, like any other teaching material, is just that—a teaching material (or a support device; e.g., hearing aid, calculator). How teachers use teaching materials determines whether their students learn, generalize, and maintain what they are taught. Providing a student with a textbook or a work sheet with a pencil does not equate to teaching. Instead, the teacher has to structure how those tools are used by the student or teacher to generate learning. Learning will not just occur in the presence of the teaching materials (technology); even with computer-assisted instruction, the teacher has to match the technology to the student's needs, plan implementation, and monitor performance.

Because technology for teaching has such a broad range, this book is organized around two general technology domains. Ayres, Shepley, Douglas, Shepley, and Lane (2016) divided technology into two categories: assistive technology (AT) and instructional technology (IT). This division roughly separates those technologies that are purposely built to teach a skill (IT) from those technologies that instead are designed to support an area of performance deficit (AT).

Assistive Technology

In 1988, Congress passed the Technology Related Assistance for Individuals with Disabilities Act (P.L. 100-407), which provided states with funding to create statewide programs for providing technology-related support for individuals with disabilities. Then, in the 1990 reauthorization of the Individuals with Disabilities Education Act (IDEA; P.L. 101-476), Congress defined assistive technology as:

> any item, piece of equipment or product system, whether acquired commercially off the shelf, modified, or customized, that is used to increase, maintain, or improve the functional capabilities of children with disabilities. The term does not include a medical device that is surgically implanted, or the replacement of such a device. (Authority 20 U.S.C. 1402(1))

This broadly encompassing definition includes everything from a voice output communication device costing several thousand dollars to a slant board made from a three-ring binder and duct tape. The service component in the 1990 reauthorization is a critical piece of the legislation because it encompasses evaluation, securing of the equipment, customization, and training for teachers, therapists, and families. The law identifies this as a service that schools need to consider.

In 1997, the law expanded to require schools to consider the role of AT in the Individualized Education Programs (IEPs) of all students and to clear the way for AT purchased by the school to be used in the home. This was an important step because it meant that, for the first time, as the IEP team met to write the IEP, they had to at least have a conversation about the role that AT might play for a student. There is no prescribed process or formal protocol for this conversation, nor is there much of any guidance from the U.S. Department of Education. Nevertheless, the requirement in the law compels the team to at least think through ways that AT may support a student's learning.

The law does not make a distinction between AT and IT. By the law, for example, software designed to provide a student with practice on math computation could be considered AT. For the purposes and organization of this book, we make the distinction because the two function differently; that is, teachers use them for different purposes. In general, this book focuses on AT as a means of support that is not designed to teach a skill but to help a learner overcome a skill or ability deficit. AT would likely remain a permanent part of that individual's life. For example, one would not generally or necessarily expect a learner to stop needing an augmentative and alternative communication (AAC) device (e.g., voice output system) as he or she ages. While AAC can be a bridge to vocal communication, users who require AAC support typically require some form of AAC for life. IT, on the other hand, is different.

Instructional Technology

Where AAC will likely be a part of an individual's life forever, this book focuses on IT as encompassing technologies that are designed to assist with teaching a skill, after which they systematically fade from the environment or teach other new skills. This process is similar to what occurs when a student works his or her way completely through a social studies textbook and has demonstrated competence in the material, and thus no longer needs the book.

The use of IT—some earlier forms were referred to as computer-assisted instruction (CAI)—has been a part of education for students with disabilities, including ASD, since the 1980s (Pennington, 2010). IT, or CAI, has been used to teach individuals with ASD reading skills (Coleman-Martin, Heller, Cihak, & Irvine, 2005), math skills (Ayres & Langone, 2002; Chen & Bernard-Opitz, 1993), content area instruction, such as map reading (McKissick, Spooner, Wood, & Diegelmann, 2013), as well as life skills (Ayres & Cihak, 2010; Charlop-Christy, Le, & Freeman, 2000). The role of IT may vary depending on the learner and teacher needs. For example, teachers may use IT to augment other instruction like in math (Bouck, Satsangi, Doughty, & Courtney, 2014). If the teacher is delivering instruction in small groups, and a student needs additional practice, software may permit the student to solve a number of problems and receive the prompting and feedback they need to make progress. Ayres, Langone, Boon, and Norman (2006) used IT to provide additional instructional trials to a group of students who needed assistance generalizing money skills from classroom simulations to the natural environment. These students had been responding correctly to trials with the teacher in tabletop activities but were not generalizing to the community. Adding IT to supplement classroom instruction resulted in the students ultimately generalizing to local stores. Alternatively, teachers may rely on software as the primary means of instruction. For example, Travers et al. (2011) evaluated the use of computer-assisted instruction as the sole means of teaching a set number of letters of the alphabet. This was contrasted with teacher-directed instruction. In both cases, students acquired the alphabet recognition skills being targeted. Regardless of whether IT is used alone or as a supplement to other instruction, the teacher should deliberately plan how the technology will be used and monitor student performance.

Some commercially available IT for learners with ASD provides ongoing performance monitoring and record keeping (e.g., DT Trainer, Accelerations Educational Software, n.d.). IT, however, relies on teacher oversight to ensure that students are making adequate progress. Many mobile applications fall into this latter category. Much of the IT that teachers create themselves also do not have the capacity to collect and store data. The bulk of this book discussing IT focuses on teacher-created IT. The reason for this focus is to make the IT portions of this book long-lasting and maximally relevant for practitioners and not out-of-date as new technology develops. Emphasizing specific current software, for example, would result in portions of the book being outdated before it is published. Because technology evolves rapidly, building a solid understanding of basic design principles will allow teachers to select commercially produced software as well as design materials customized to their students. Given the range of needs that students with ASD have, and the necessity of crafting individualized instruction, teachers with skill in designing instructional materials can use common presentation tools (e.g., PowerPoint, Keynote, or Slides) to develop customized IT.

This book is organized around an initial discussion and overview of technology in the classroom learning environment. Following this, the discussion shifts to examining how to select technology, implement technology supports, design instructional technology, and monitor implementation. The chapters directly focused on using technology include a series of case studies that build across the chapters and provide examples for how to approach using technology. Most of the case studies include data sheets that help to illustrate how a teacher or therapist might track student learning or use of the technology. These can be easily re-created using a word processor. (See Appendix A for examples of data sheets.)

REVIEW QUESTIONS
1. Differentiate AT and IT.
2. Provide two examples of AT.
3. Provide two examples of IT.

DISCUSSION QUESTIONS
1. Identify one piece of technology that supports your day-to-day life and discuss how the demands on your time or abilities would be different without this technology.
2. Identify a piece of instructional technology that you learned from while in elementary or middle school. Discuss how learning from that technology was a different experience from learning from a classroom lecture.

2 Types of Technology in the Learning Environment

Before we discuss how to select or design technology solutions for classrooms, the reader should first have some familiarity with the range of technology available. The emphasis in this chapter is not so much on specific models or brands but more on different types of technology and their utility for supporting learning. By increasing familiarity with the types of technology, an educator will be better prepared to contribute to the technology selection and planning for a given student. Readers should not consider this an exhaustive encyclopedia of technology; rather, the reader should consider this chapter a survey of some AT and IT solutions. The goal is to provide the reader, new to AT and IT, with a general sense of the types of technology available. The book could not possibly catalog all available technology for multiple reasons. First, with commercial technology innovations, new products are always being developed and coming to market. Second, in a similar vein, specifically with IT, teachers and other practitioners frequently find ways to exploit off-the-shelf technology in beneficial ways that exceed what the designers originally intended (more on this later). Lastly, in the area of AT, the range of items—from pencil grips to slant boards to visual timers and computer software—could, in theory, encompass nearly any tangible thing in a classroom, depending on how it is used.

Assistive Technology

Augmentative and Alternative Communication

Likely the most prominent role for AT in the life of a child or youth with autism or ASD is augmentative and alternative communication (AAC). Technology in this realm covers a broad range of systems, from low-tech solutions like Picture Exchange Communication System (PECS) or a small white board, to advanced, tablet-based communication systems. Given that this book is about technology, we will not focus on unaided AAC-like sign language, but rather examine some of the technology available for aided AAC.

Beginning with nonelectronic options, one of the most common AAC solutions for communication involves the use of pictures (photos, line drawings, cartoons) that students point to or give to a communication partner. The basic process of using images as a communication aid has existed in special education for decades. (Blissymbols came into prominence in the 1970s, for example.) The most common systematic, picture-based communication system used today is likely

PECS (Bondy & Frost, 1994). The PECS protocol involves more than just giving a child a book with strips of Velcro to which a teacher attaches laminated pictures. In practice, one will frequently find students for whom adults report "we tried PECS, but it did not work." Upon further investigation, one often realizes that a student was just given a book filled with pictures and did not receive systematic training. This book does not detail the entirety of the PECS training protocol. Readers who believe they work with children who would benefit from this type of communication system are encouraged to pursue training and implement the protocol with fidelity.

In terms of electronic communication options, educators can consider simple single-button voice output communication devices (VOCAs) like a Big Mac, multi-button devices like a GoTalks, or more advanced systems that are either stand-alone dedicated devices like DynaVox or software applications for tablets such as Proloquo2go or AutisMate. On the simple end, with single switches (generally a large colored button measuring approximately 2–3 inches in diameter), users have a limited range of messages they can communicate, but the button serves as a very clear signal for them to press without the need for them to discriminate it from other messages. Users just need to push the button, and a recorded message is played. Teachers can include more than a single button to provide more communication options. Likewise, advancing to devices with multiple buttons increases the opportunities for a student to engage. With these lower tech devices the teacher has to record the message for each button. In terms of social validity, if the teacher is recording the audio for the buttons, he or she should consider the age and gender of the child for whom the device will be used. This device is the child's voice—and a 5-year-old boy's voice probably should not sound like a 35-year-old woman's voice. Seeking out typically developing peers of the same gender and age to record the messages can provide the student with a more appropriate-sounding voice.

On the higher tech end, the dedicated devices and software function more like a computer interface, providing an array of user options for selecting and building messages. These can range from hitting a single button to deliver a single message to pairing buttons to speak in unique and complete sentences, or even typing out a comment on a keyboard. For each of these options, high-tech devices provide the user with a communication system that can closely replicate spoken communication.

Environmental Access

One of the other ways that students with ASD often use AT is to physically access their environment. This book does not go into depth on the material adaptations for all areas of environmental access (e.g., specialized plates and bowls); however, we do discuss environmental access as it relates to computers. For some learners, a mouse and keyboard serve as a barrier to accessing computer technology. In such cases, touch screens become an obvious solution (one feature that makes tablets popular). Additionally, there are other computer adaptations to consider, as well as accessibility options built into the operating systems of Windows and OS X. Some of the more common add-on solutions include adaptive keyboards (which have oversized keys or keys arranged in alphabetical order and without the extra function keys) and key guards that allow users to rest their hands on the keyboard without having to hover them over the keys. For users with more limited mobility, a range of switches or single-button controls is available that will allow computer interaction. Likewise, if students have very limited mobility of their limbs, they can access their computer via eye gaze to operate a mouse and on-screen keyboard. For users who have good vocal communication skills, a variety of ways exist for them to control computers and tablets through voice command. It is important to keep in mind that the integration of voice command into specific software will be limited by and need to be in accordance with the software itself.

Educational Assistive Technology

We have shared some of the ways users can interact with computers and tablets with AT supports. Once a user has access to a computer, there are a number of AT options that teachers might consider in order to remove other barriers to learning with technology. Two areas where AT can play a very important role in academics are reading and writing. In terms of reading, electronic text can provide a user with a range of supports to aid in comprehension. From text-to-speech, whereby the user is able to listen and follow along with the text, to texts enhanced with quick links to definitions, explanations, supplemental images, and so on, technology can provide supports as the user needs them. Many of these features teachers may already have familiarity with if they read e-books via Kindle or other platforms. The National Center for Supported Electronic Text (http://ncset .uoregon.edu) is an invaluable asset for identifying electronic text resources. In cases where teachers have to modify text to change readability and increase the numbers of supports available for a student, the Center for Applied Special Technology Bookbuilder platform (http://bookbuilder.cast.org) allows teachers to generate materials that have the electronic support their students need. Another resource for teachers seeking accessible digital materials to integrate into instruction is the National Center on Accessible Educational Materials (NCAEM; http:// aem.cast.org). While NCAEM has a broad mission, including sensory and physical impairments, it can provide teachers with additional ideas and resources for supporting learners with ASD.

For students with ASD who struggle with handwriting, providing them the option to type instead of write by hand can serve as an AT that increases their writing output. Another alternative, for learners with slow typing skills and fine motor deficits that make handwriting and typing poor options, is for the student to use speech-to-text or dictation technologies. Current word processor/operating systems have fairly workable options built in, but dedicated software solutions are available as well. Some students may not have difficulty with the motor aspects of typing but struggle more with organizing ideas, spelling, sentence construction, word retrieval, and so on, which make composing essays very challenging. In these instances, teachers should consider some of the writing support software options available on the market that provide tools such as built-in graphic organizers, word prediction, and text-to-speech reading to assist with proofing papers.

AT math supports for students are also available. The simplest and most common support is a calculator. When a student has an educational goal to solve complex multi-step math problems (e.g., quadratic equations) that require basic arithmetic like addition and subtraction, and he or she has already mastered the mechanics and concepts of arithmetic but takes a long time to compute the answers, using a calculator can reduce barriers by helping increase speed and fluency related to the basic calculations. Likewise, manipulatives, number lines, and other visual supports can be incorporated as low-tech AT to assist learners with ASD in visualizing mathematical concepts and operations. The Mathematics eText Research Center (http://metrc.uoregon.edu) provides some of the best resources for teachers looking at options to support learners struggling with the print aspects of math.

This brief overview provides context for the discussions in later chapters regarding the selection and use of AT. To be sure, readers should note that this is a much abbreviated survey of AT available for learners with ASD and is intended to provide the uninitiated and neophyte reader some idea of what types of resources are available. Readers seeking more in-depth information on specific technologies are encouraged to peruse the peer-reviewed literature and examine other textbooks dedicated to covering AT in depth.

Instructional Technology

This section differs from the approach in the AT section. Instead of covering multiple categories of IT, this section focuses on key features teachers should consider when selecting or designing IT for their students. Commercially produced IT is available to support instruction in all academic areas, as well as in social skills and life skills. Whereas a decade ago classrooms accessed most IT on CDs, today much of the technology is web-based or app-based on mobile devices. An emerging area of IT is augmented reality, which can bridge the categories of AT and IT but for which there is scant research evidence currently to support it as a technology solution for individuals with ASD. Rather than attempting to catalog all IT available on the market, this section focuses on where the research evidence has documented quantifiable growth and improved learning outcomes. Not all IT will lead to learning improvements for every student with ASD, and some IT options will be unacceptable. There are a lot of options available that some might derisively call "edu-tainment." As the market for personal computers expanded in the 1980s and 1990s, software developers began creating a range of titles targeted at parents and schools with the promise of making learning more fun and exciting. Many of those games failed to produce the types of measurable learning gains that would warrant using instructional time to play. Therefore, this section approaches the discussion of IT conservatively and focuses on the key evidence-based instructional elements that teachers should consider in IT rather than specific titles. Even if a specific software title does not have research supporting it, if the underlying instructional methods do, then teachers should consider how and if it would benefit their students. By having a general idea of ways IT can assist in instruction and the features to look for, teachers can better incorporate IT to augment their instruction. To facilitate this discussion, IT is broken broadly into IT designed to improve discrete skills and IT designed to build multi-step chained skills.

An important area of IT for individuals with ASD relates to teacher-, parent-, and therapist-created content. In 1996, Higgins and Boone wrote about the ways that teachers could use multimedia authoring software to create customized learning materials for individuals with ASD. At that time, HyperCard and Hyper-Studio were two powerful yet simple tools that teachers and researchers were using to develop materials (e.g., Mechling, Gast, & Langone, 2002; Simpson, Langone, & Ayres, 2004). While such software is no longer available, current presentation software programs like PowerPoint can do many of the same things. Customized IT developed by teachers and designed to address specific student needs can better reflect the environment in which the learner lives. Mechling, Ayres, Foster, and Bryant (2013) reported results of a study showing that a group of high school students with ASD learned a set of life skills more rapidly and completely through instructional materials designed to reflect their environment than they did from a similar set of commercially produced IT materials. Later in this book we turn our attention to exploring some of the ways to create customized technologies.

Discrete Skill Acquisition and Fluency Building

Regardless of content area, one of the most basic ways that teachers can incorporate IT into instruction is by identifying software that provides students with increased opportunities to respond. In general, increasing active student responding or opportunities to learn has been associated with increased academic gains (e.g., MacSuga-Gage & Simonsen, 2015; Schnorr, Freeman-Green, & Test, 2016). Software provides an ideal context for these increased response opportunities because software can tirelessly present more learning trials and feedback to students. Frequently criticized as "drill and practice" types of programs, well-designed software that prompts and corrects a learner can provide a level of intensive one-on-one instruction beyond what a teacher might normally be able to offer.

When evaluating software in this area, teachers should consider a few questions. First, how well does the software align with the curriculum? For some content areas, software alignment will not be an issue (e.g., an app that provides fluency training on multiplication). For other areas (e.g., history related), material presented in the software may not cover the content sufficiently or may provide additional content beyond what the student needs to learn (thus overwhelming the learner or distracting from the key objectives). Does the software provide sufficient exemplars to promote generalization? Ideally, the software should provide the teacher with ways to customize or control the difficulty and scope of the content delivered. For example, if the content area is sight vocabulary, the ideal software should allow control over the words and the number of different words in a learning set. Well-designed software should also provide a feedback mechanism that promotes learning by correcting errors and telling the student when he or she responds correctly. Ideally, the software should also provide some level of prompting to decrease trial-and-error learning (or guessing) on the part of the student. Finally, software designed in the tradition of computer-assisted instruction (CAI) will document student progress and provide teachers with information on student responding. As the student improves, the software can manage the difficulty and advance the learner along.

Key Questions for Evaluating Software for Skill Acquisition and Fluency

1. How well does the software align with the curriculum?
2. Does the software provide sufficient exemplars to promote generalization?
3. Does the software provide a feedback mechanism or prompting?
4. How does the software document student progress and information on student responding?

Multi-Step and Chained Tasks

Frequently teachers take complex tasks (from algebra to doing dishes) and break them down for instruction into discrete or multi-step chained tasks as a way of sequencing required responses. Essay writing involves, for example, sequencing multiple sentences and building paragraphs around a series of facts or premises. This is in contrast to single, discrete academic responses that might require a student to identify the dominant religions of Asia. While dividing academic and learning content into two simple categories may seem to provide an overly simplistic dichotomy, it provides a very basic way to approach teaching complex responding. Solving a quadratic equation or describing a chemical reaction involves multiple, sequenced steps. Likewise, actions such as learning to tie a shoe or making a purchase at a grocery store comprise a series of smaller steps. Most of the research on teaching chained tasks with software has focused on teaching targets in the area of life skills with video modeling or video prompting. The majority of this work relied on very simple uses of IT to help support student learning.

There is supporting evidence that teachers looking for software to support instruction of multi-stepped chains should consider custom-made IT as the best solution (Mechling, 2005). Some research exists on the efficacy of commercially produced software to mimic natural environments and provide a virtual context for learning (e.g., Ayres & Cihak, 2010; Hutcherson, Langone, Ayres, & Clees, 2004); however, the simplest solution for most teachers will be to create materials to support instruction. Unlike the discrete-trial types of technology discussed in the previous section, which directly prompt and provide corrective feedback, the IT used to teach chained tasks most frequently involves some type of teacher mediation. Essentially, most video prompting or picture prompting research has evaluated technology as an adjunct to teacher-directed instruction, where the technology serves as a medium for prompting. For example, consider a teacher who is teaching a student to cook and wants to model the step of turning the dial for a burner on the range. If the teacher has only one range to use to model the step, he or she must turn the dial on and then turn it off again so that the student can have an opportunity to imitate the step. If the student imitates exactly what he or she saw modeled, he or she will turn the burner on and then off (not the desired outcome). Instead, by using video prompting, the teacher can show a video model that exactly matches the desired response.

Additionally, whereas software that focuses on discrete skills involves responding almost exclusively in the software itself (on the computer, tablet, etc.), software that teaches chained skills tends to involve responding elsewhere in the environment (e.g., in natural contexts), as shown by the bulk of research. In some ways this may make the technology look more like AT (i.e., supporting responding rather than teaching specific behaviors). However, self-instructional literature researchers have reported that users self-fade the technology as they become more proficient in the skills (Sigafoos et al., 2007; Smith et al., 2016). Given the research on customized instructional materials for teaching chained multi-step responding, teachers should likely first consider creating their own materials that reflect the learner's environment and related idiosyncratic features and needs. Later in this book we look at a few ways to design instructional tools to support teaching chained tasks and some of the software tools that can assist teachers in the design and use of technology for this purpose.

Additional Key Questions for Evaluating Software for Skill Acquisition and Fluency

1. Does the target skill require multiple steps/behaviors?
2. Where should the target skill be performed?
3. Do the steps of the target skill have to be performed in a specific order?

REVIEW QUESTIONS

1. Identify two ways that AT can be used to increase an individual's access to his or her environment.
2. What are key factors that teachers should look for when selecting software to teach discrete responses?
3. Most of the research on IT to teach multi-stepped responses measures the learner's response in what context? How does this differ from the work on IT focused on discrete skills?

DISCUSSION QUESTIONS

1. How is software similar to and different from older educational technology, such as textbooks?
2. What are some reasons that custom-designed IT may lead to better outcomes than commercially produced IT?
3. Suppose a teacher is looking at a specific (fictional) software program called The Most Amazing Math Game. The teacher has scoured the research but has not identified a single study evaluating The Most Amazing Math Game. In what cases might the teacher be able to incorporate this game into instruction and still be able to say that he or she is using only evidence-based practice?

3 Selecting Technology for the Learning Environment

The role of technology is not to teach; rather, technology's role is to assist with teaching. Students may learn from technology just as they learn from a textbook (and now many textbooks are electronic), but the teacher needs to carefully select the technology, plan for implementation, structure opportunities to use the technology, train students to use the technology, and monitor the impact. The teacher's expertise with technology will dictate in part how much the students learn using the technology (IT) and the extent to which the technology allows more independent engagement (AT). Too often, inexperienced educators default to relying on technology to teach and fail to realize the importance of their role as the primary architect of the educational environment. Experienced teachers understand the need to organize day-to-day instructional opportunities to maximize learning and that technology can play a role in increasing the number of positive and beneficial learning trials a student has in a given day.

Knowing about available AT and IT is one variable that helps the teacher or therapist consider how to integrate the technology. The depth of the teacher's knowledge of and experience with the technology also contributes to his or her ability to successfully integrate it into the student's instructional programming and environment. The technology and instructional context (e.g., general education classroom with 25 students versus special education classroom with 6 students versus a one-on-one therapeutic environment) also influence AT and IT application and integration.

In school contexts where paraprofessionals frequently provide direct instruction or in places where assistant therapists may take over primary instructional duties, the quality of their training and their familiarity with the technology will also influence how well it is integrated. Taking this training and experience into consideration when planning for AT and IT use will assist the team in ensuring high degrees of procedural fidelity. This chapter focuses on general issues for preparing to use technology in the classroom. Later these topics are discussed in more detail relative to specific technologies.

Selecting Technology

Before selecting technology to use as AT in a classroom, the teacher needs to consider the purpose that technology needs to serve. The selection of appropriate technology (AT or IT) should come from a team-based process that includes the learner. In addition to the student, his or her parents, and the teacher, other important team members might include speech pathologists, occupational or physical therapists, and certainly the assistive technology experts who are available in some school districts. In terms of the learner, he or she may or may not have the ability to orally tell the team what technologies he or she prefers, but by including the learner in this process and allowing him or her to engage with the technology, the team can begin to ascertain whether the technology is likely to be an appropriate fit. If the learner is able to share his or her thoughts with the team, these need careful consideration. For example, if the team is making a recommendation for a technology that the student feels would be stigmatizing, then he or she is more likely to abandon it (Parette & Scherer, 2004; Watts, O'Brian, & Wojcik, 2004).

Several formal models exist for guiding teams through the AT decision-making process. One example of these models is the SETT Framework (Zabala, 1995). SETT stands for Student, Environment, Tasks, and Tools; it leads the team through a series of questions designed to focus attention on the student and expectations of the environment. Detailed examples of the framework, including handouts, can be found at www.joyzabala.com. Another example is from the National Assistive Technology Research Institute (www.natri.uky.edu), which provides a framework for planning implementation that helps guide a team through examining the student's needs relative to the learning environment. The existing models have a common theme related to ensuring that the technology matches

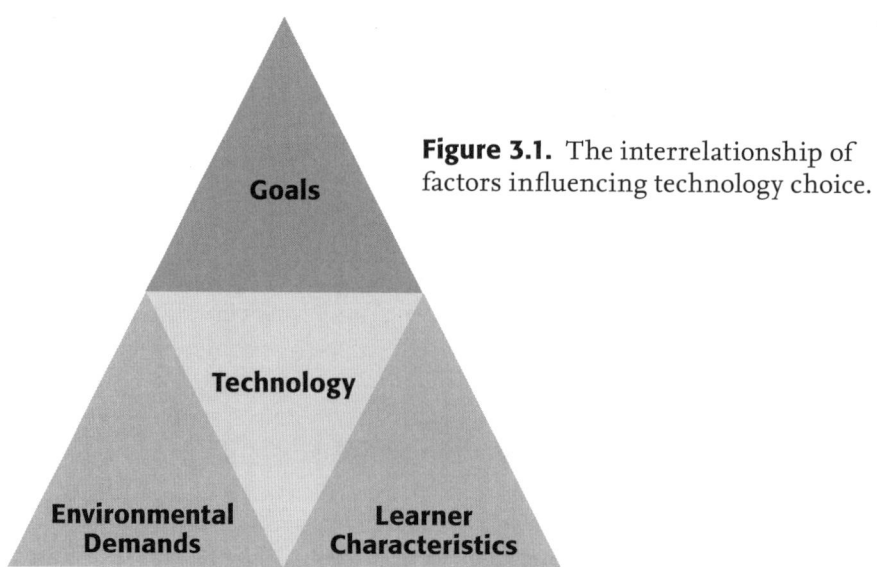

Figure 3.1. The interrelationship of factors influencing technology choice.

Goals

Technology

Environmental Demands

Learner Characteristics

the environmental context: where it will be used and whether it assists the needs of the student relative to that context.

Our intention in this book is not to oversimplify these frameworks. Entire books can be written about them; thus the focus here is on a few key elements. This chapter focuses on selecting technology and probing the use of it. The following chapter will discuss implementation issues and monitoring the effects. Figure 3.1 illustrates how these components fit together, with the aim of supporting the learner in achieving his or her goals. Table 3.1 places these goals in the context of real-life examples. The technology bridges the gap between the learner and the contextual demands leading to progress.

Table 3.1. Real-Life Examples of the Factors Influencing Technology Choice

	Identify goals	Environmental demands	Learner skills	Technology options
Defined	Specify learning outcomes that technology may support.	Pinpoint how technology will support instruction (IT) or engagement (AT).	Detail learner skills relative to the technology.	
AT example	Maurice will spontaneously request toys or activities during free play when access to those items is restricted.	Technology will support Maurice's communication by providing a consistent means of communication in the play area. It will also provide an auditory alternative to him pointing and allow him to appropriately gain the attention of adults and peers.	Maurice can discriminate from a field of four or more objects and pictures. He can isolate a single finger for pointing. He gestures for things he wants.	• PECS • Big Mac • 4-button AAC
IT example	Jamari will tell time to 5-minute increments on digital and analog clocks.	Technology is needed to provide multiple exemplars, as well as response and stimulus prompting and corrective feedback.	Jamari will work independently for periods of up to 20 minutes. He can manipulate a mouse and a touch screen.	• Web-based options • Teacher-generated lessons • Tablet apps

Step 1. Define goals.

To effectively select AT or design IT for a student, the team first has to explicitly identify the goals for integrating technology. What will the technology do to help the student learn content or access materials or their environment? For example, a student who needs more opportunities to respond on basic math content might benefit from certain sorts of IT. Another student might require technology to help him or her communicate. By outlining clear objectives, the team will avoid pursuing technologies just for the sake of having technology. Whether evaluating AT or IT, the team should be able to identify what the technology will do to help a student learn or perform some type of task. An AT goal for a student with communication needs might look like this: Jordan will spontaneously comment on aspects of his environment. Teams can draw goals specifically from a student's IEP, as in the previous example, or they may tailor the goals such that they do not specifically link to any explicit IEP objective. For example, a student might have IEP objectives around specific academic content. However, the goal selected by the technology team might be relatively general: Amir will compose a paragraph-long answer with the assistance of AT.

When planning to use IT to help students achieve academic goals, the team should consider whether the goals focus more on acquisition, fluency, generalization, or maintenance. In the beginning phases of acquisition, the teacher may put more weight on whether the IT provides quality prompting and feedback. If the goal is related to generalization, then emphasis on the number of learning exemplars presented may take priority. For fluency-related goals, the ability of the IT to track rate becomes important in assisting teachers to monitor impact. When teachers target maintenance, they may find ways to integrate any IT used for acquisition, fluency, or generalization.

Regardless of whether a team plans to add AT or IT to a student's program, specific and clear goals with an accompanying timeline will assist a team in knowing when the individual has achieved an objective and whether the selected technology has helped the child accomplish his or her goals. Setting a time parameter for when the student should achieve the goal will further assist the team because it provides for a clear decision point on reevaluating the effects of the technology. For example, if a child simply needs more opportunities to practice a specific academic task, the team can identify a fluency goal for the student and pursue IT that will assist the student with achieving that objective. If the student achieves that objective in the specified time frame, the team has learned that the specific IT they selected is appropriate for that student and that goal. If the student does not achieve the objective or has shown little progress toward that objective, the team knows they need to find other solutions.

After defining the goals, the team needs to move on to considering the student's characteristics.

Step 2. Identify the individual's strengths and weaknesses.

For an individual to use the technology effectively and efficiently, it is important to determine his or her strengths and deficits and match these to the qualities of the technology. Knowing the learner's present level of ability and knowing general characteristics of that learner (e.g., has difficulty with fine motor control), the teacher will have the information needed to identify the most appropriate technology solutions. This is true for AT as well as IT. For example, not every child needs to have a touch screen AAC device just because he or she is not speaking. A young child who has not yet begun to discriminate the cause and effect of his or her behavior on his or her environment and cannot isolate one finger to touch a 1-inch by 1-inch square in an array of 24 squares is not likely to find success with more advanced AAC and may initially benefit from very simple micro-switches. Likewise, from an IT standpoint, if a learner has demonstrated mastery of academic content and uses that information regularly (e.g., addition and subtraction), then drill and practice software covering this material will not likely help the learner improve unless he or she has a specific goal for fluency that he or she has not yet met.

For a young child whose communication skills are emerging and who is relying primarily on gross gestures to signal wants and needs, an initial communication objective might involve a simple switch press (without discriminating between switches). In this case, the teacher would work with the child's speech therapist to identify appropriate micro-switches. Often the selection options to test are limited by what the school has available. In such cases, trying different options and monitoring student performance may be the route that is required. A small, flat switch (¼-inch thick and 1½ inches in diameter) may not provide a salient enough target for a young child just beginning to use AAC. In this instance, a much larger switch (3 inches thick and 3 inches in diameter) may be more conspicuous and a better starting point.

In terms of IT, an understanding of the learner's strengths and weaknesses helps the team select appropriate software as well. For example, if a student tends to learn better from a visual presentation of information rather than auditory, having software that doesn't rely on audio instructions but instead makes sure that all communication with the users gets displayed on the screen in either text or pictures makes sense. If a learner struggles with typing or simply is too young to reasonably be expected to type, then IT that allows the user to respond via a mouse or touch screen to most activities would permit better engagement than a program that requires the user to type all responses.

Step 3. Identify the demands of the environment.

Frequently teams generally only think of environmental demands in relation to AT that helps provide access to some aspect of the environment or instructional setting. For example, in a language arts class, a teacher might expect the learners to interact with text and write. For a learner who has difficulty with fine motor control or attending, the AT should address these needs. This might mean that instructional materials are arranged such that the student does not have to manipulate pages and that the text (if electronic) provides frequent prompts for the student to respond to comprehension questions. Similarly, relative to communication and AT, one of the environmental demands to consider in an elementary school environment would involve how the student communicates during physical education (PE) and recess. That is, is the device lightweight and mobile, and does it permit shared and reciprocal interactions among peers? In relation to IT, the demands of the environment have more to do with the curriculum content and the match between the curriculum content and the IT.

If a teacher uses software to support other instruction, then making sure that the software and the stimuli within the software align with what the student encounters in the rest of his or her instructional environment will help with generalization. For acquisition objectives, the teacher needs to identify or create IT that matches the content of the learning objectives. While this may seem like an obvious requirement, if a student has an objective related to learning about the U.S. electoral college and the teacher uses an online game that generally covers presidential elections but does not explicitly address the learning standards, the teacher will have to augment that lesson with additional curricula. If teachers create their own materials, they have greater control over the content and can ensure that their students engage with all of the material related to the objectives. Similarly, if a young student practices letter identification or letter-sound correspondence on software that presents letters only in a sans-serif font (where a lowercase letter *g* might have an open curve at the bottom that opens to the left in contrast to a lowercase *g* that looks almost like two separate circles connected by a small line in Times New Roman), the student may have difficulty generalizing to other materials. On the other hand, this may provide an opportunity for multiple-exemplar training with the explicit goal of enhancing generalization across stimuli.

Step 4. Identify technology options.

At this stage, the team needs to invest time in exploring possible technology solutions. Relying on a single person to identify options may limit the potential of the team to find an optimal solution. Each team member has expertise to contribute. Speech therapists have extensive training in a range of communication technologies and occupational therapists have backgrounds in identifying adaptive solutions related to fine motor control. Teachers frequently have more extensive backgrounds in curriculum and related technologies. Parents and students can also contribute because they often network with other families who have explored similar issues. Moreover, the needs of a family's child are clearly very particular and personal, and the family's investment in that child's progress will likely exceed that of others. Therefore, the time they have spent searching for solutions will benefit the team in brainstorming options. Some school systems also employ dedicated AT experts. Even if the district does not have such a person, it frequently has a designated person who tracks the AT for the district. This means that that person likely has a good working knowledge of what the district has available, as well as what students in the district currently and historically have used. This will help the team quickly figure out what technology they can test with the student immediately rather than having to wait for a purchase to arrive or for acquisition of a demonstration or loaner device.

In relation to IT, the team needs to again consider the goals as they pursue purchasing or designing software options. A student flipping through a set of digital flashcards built using PowerPoint that provide no corrective feedback for errors or acknowledgment of correct responses is unlikely to effectively learn. These are two components that teachers can design into their own materials and are covered in a later chapter. In trying to build a generalized responding repertoire for a skill like receptive identification, IT provides a platform where a range of multiple exemplars can be easily incorporated. Whether teachers are searching for commercially produced IT or creating it themselves, sampling the range of target stimuli becomes an important part of programming for generalization.

Frequently the educational team will not know the perfect option and should consider multiple technologies for a trial implementation. Identifying a range of possible options based on goals, needs, and skills will provide the team with a starting point to test the technology with each learner. If the team approaches this phase with an open mind and does not prematurely pinpoint or single out a specific technology (or technology at all), the members can make an objective decision based on the student interaction with the technology and his or her environment.

As is the case with AT, by identifying several options based on a student's objectives, needs, and abilities, the education team can test and probe technology to see what fits best for a specific learner. This will help ensure that the student uses the most appropriate technology and not just what was available for the team. Moreover, the testing process may reveal that the learner lacks some of the prerequisite skills required to navigate the software (e.g., does not have a high enough reading level) or that the software may be too unengaging (boring) to meet the learner's needs.

Step 5. Test the technology fit.

Whether the search is for AT or IT solutions, making sure that the learner has an opportunity to inform that process is important. Frequently, for learners whose communication skills prohibit them from contributing substantively to discussions on the technology, the education team will have to rely on observations of the learner's interaction with technology. For AT, this might involve several sessions of the learner practicing with the different technologies, with the teacher gauging the student's comfort. During this process, the teacher will likely have to provide some preliminary instruction on how to use the technology. Then, for example, if using an AAC strategy, the teacher might count the number of independent or prompted uses, the level of student attention, or how frequently the learner independently approaches the technology. The teacher should also consider measuring any undesirable behavior, such as pushing away the technology, throwing it, or producing negative vocalizations. Similarly, with AT designed to support higher level academics, even if the student can tell the teacher what he or she does and does not like, observation of the student using multiple text prediction programs while writing may help guide the team toward the best solution. With regard to IT, a similar process is warranted. With commercially produced IT, the teacher may download a trial version or borrow the program from another teacher to allow a student to try it. The teacher can record similar observations (e.g., level of engagement, required adult prompting). Just because a user does not gravitate immediately toward the technology does not mean that the teacher needs to abandon it. Rather, this information can inform how the student is taught to use the technology. It becomes one more variable a teacher needs to consider when deciding how to move forward.

In sum, the process of selecting (or developing) technology is a deliberate activity where the teacher and other members of the education team consider the explicit learning objectives for each student. They then match those objectives and the student's needs to suitable technology. Focusing the process on goals and outcomes will hopefully reduce incorporating technology for the sake of technology while also improving integration and learner performance. Identifying and objectively testing options may take time, but it will decrease the likelihood of a mismatch in technology and learner resulting from the educational team's less-than-fully-informed guesses. Given scarce resources, educational teams that proceed in a planful manner will maximize their efficiency and better meet the needs of all of their students. The next chapter proceeds into technology implementation and monitoring.

Steps of the Technology Selection Process

1. Define the goals for the technology.
2. Identify the strengths and weaknesses of the learner.
3. Identify the demands of the environment.
4. List the options.
5. Test the technology fit.

REVIEW QUESTIONS

1. What is meant by the idea of matching a technology to a learner and his or her environment?
2. What is meant by probing or testing technology? Why is this important?

DISCUSSION QUESTION

1. Why should the learner be a part of the educational decision-making team? What if the learner has very limited communication skills and may not be able to tell the team about his or her wants and needs? How can the team still take the learner's opinions into account?

Jack and AAC

Jack is a 6-year-old boy in the first grade. He uses three spoken words (*hi, mom*, and *no*) and several word approximations, but does not use them reliably in the classroom or home setting. When he wants or needs something, he will often point or pull someone's hand toward the object. He gets upset when he cannot clearly communicate to an adult what he wants and will begin crying and often hitting the adult. He rarely interacts with peers in class or on the playground.

Jack's parents and the speech pathologist agree that Jack would benefit from some type of AAC support. The team's long-term goal for Jack is for him to communicate with people in his environment with speech using full sentences to make requests, carry on conversations, respond to questions, and so forth. In the short term, however, the primary goal for Jack is the following: Within 2 months, Jack will spontaneously request at least three different preferred objects in his environment when he cannot independently access them (e.g., popcorn, milk, and puzzles). Related to this goal, his parents and speech pathologist considered single-button switches as well as tablet-based options. His environment dictated that he needed to communicate multiple messages, and he has the fine motor ability necessary to interact on an iPad. To begin, his teacher decided to probe to see what he could do. When she placed two images in front of him, one of his favorite snack (popcorn) and one of a pencil (not a preferred item), Jack repeatedly picked the image on his right, even when it was the pencil. After this occurred across several days and several different images of preferred and nonpreferred items, his teacher determined that he was not able to discriminate between the images. For this reason, his teacher decided to start teaching Jack PECS, beginning with phase 1 (i.e., exchanging an icon of a preferred item for the actual item). The objective of this goal was to work up through phases 2 and 3 of PECS to teach Jack discrimination of the images while simultaneously giving him a means to request the things he wants and needs.

Dante and Environmental Access

Dante is a 10-year-old boy in the third grade who has ASD and cerebral palsy. He has no deficits in speech (no one has difficulty understanding him), but physical disabilities limit his gross and fine motor skills. Dante independently uses a wheelchair, but an aide accompanies him throughout the school day to assist in toileting and other physical tasks (e.g., moving objects from one location to another, eating). Academically, Dante performs at grade level, but he often cannot physically complete assignments and needs a scribe for work in math and reading that requires writing.

In language arts, his class will be working on creative writing this year, and his teacher discovered that Dante excels at creating original, detailed stories. Although Dante cannot write, his teacher believes that he can independently access the writing curriculum by using a computer to compose his narratives. The team's goal for Dante was the following: Within 4 months Dante will compose a three-paragraph story with no more than two errors in grammar or spelling. After talking with his parents and the occupational therapist, the team decided to try using a touch screen computer with a large, on-screen keyboard. Dante worked with the occupational therapist for a week learning to use the touch screen and practice writing using the keyboard. Although he was able to record his stories, Dante told his teacher that he found the typing tedious and tiring and often took so long he would forget his story ideas.

After Dante shared his thoughts on the touch screen technology, the teacher talked with the IEP team and decided to try speech-to-text technology. The teacher felt strongly about Dante having access to the computer so he could independently access the grade-level writing curriculum. She and other members of the IEP team felt that with Dante's strong language skills and the physical challenge of typing, a speech-to-text application would be the best method to aid him in utilizing the technology.

Case Study 3.3 — Sophie and Learning From Technology

Sophie is a 4-year-old girl in prekindergarten who received a diagnosis of ASD before starting school. She communicates in two- to three-word phrases and independently requests preferred items and needs (e.g., *open, bathroom, help, go*). To increase Sophie's communication skills, her teacher targeted expressive identification of verbs. Specifically, her teacher set the following goal: When presented with an image depicting a verb and the question "What is he doing?," Sophie will expressively identify the verb (e.g., *throwing, playing*). When the teacher presented an array of images representing verbs, Sophie independently selected the correct verb when her teacher said, "Touch _____." However, when the teacher presented a single image and asked, "What is he doing?," Sophie stated another feature of the image. For example, when presented with an image of a boy in a red shirt jumping and the question "What is he doing?," Sophie always said, "Red shirt" rather than "Jumping."

Sophie's teacher remembered a book she read in college that taught her how to use PowerPoints in discrete trial instruction. The teacher created PowerPoint slides with animated images, or GIFs, of individuals engaging in activities corresponding with the target verbs. The teacher then downloaded the PowerPoint file to the classroom iPad and used it at Sophie's workstation to display the slides one at a time and ask, "What is he doing?" She used the same procedures she used to teach Sophie still images of verbs. At first, Sophie grabbed for the iPad or said "Angry birds" each time her teacher brought it out to show the PowerPoint slides. Sophie's teacher learned how to set the iPad to Guided Access in case Sophie touched the screen or home button during discrete trial instruction. Using this function precluded Sophie's exiting the instructional slides. Once Sophie's touching the iPad did not grant her access to her favorite iPad games, she stopped reaching for the device and began attending to the slides. After several trials, the teacher felt that Sophie was more attentive when presented with the moving images and that the target feature (the action) was more salient.

Case Study Questions

1. Why would Jack's technology team want to establish a goal for him to make three different requests for objects? Why not just one?
2. Why would Jack's technology team set a timeline of 2 months for him to achieve this goal?
3. What are some of the other pragmatic challenges Dante's teacher might face in creating an environment for him to use speech-to-text software in the classroom? (Hint: Think about what Dante has to do to engage the technology with 20 to 25 other students in the classroom.) What are some ways his teacher can overcome these challenges?
4. Why might Sophie have responded to her teacher's questions by labeling features of the images rather than saying the verb?
5. How should Sophie's teacher plan for generalization? In other words, what else should Sophie's teacher do to help her acquire this skill?

4 Planning Implementation and Monitoring Effects

After completing the technology selection process, including testing the fit between the learner and the technology, the teacher needs to train the learner to use the technology. It is important to keep in mind that some of this training is frequently needed during the testing period. The final step involves monitoring implementation and assessing learner progress. Figure 4.1 illustrates this sequential process, from defining goals and learner characteristics to monitoring. This schema clearly highlights that the team's work does not end with implementation. To maximize instructional efficiency, the team has to monitor and evaluate student performance to continually gauge whether they have found the proper fit between the technology, the student, and the environmental demands.

When a team invests time and money in technology, they want to know whether their investment helped learners achieve their goals. They do not want to see users (or the rest of the team) abandon the technology. Researchers have focused significant attention on abandonment of technology, in particular AAC. Fager, Hux, Beukelman, and Karantounis (2006) reported that frequently users stopped using AAC because the support they received from teachers, therapists, and so forth diminished. Desai, Chow, Mumford, Hotze, and Chau (2014) highlighted the importance of staff training in relation to the technology to reduce abandonment. Further, they suggested that some motivational issues on the part of the staff and communication partners contributed to the rate of abandonment. The underlying logic linked to this research likely extends to other technology beyond AAC. That is, if staff stops preparing and otherwise supporting the technology and establishing appropriate contexts for the technology use, then the user will likely not have a chance to benefit from it. By training the user to use the technology, staff in the user's environment will have an opportunity to see benefits. Ideally, the early successes with the technology will reinforce continued staff support. In sum, this process begins with training, and staff training is key to sustainability and generalization.

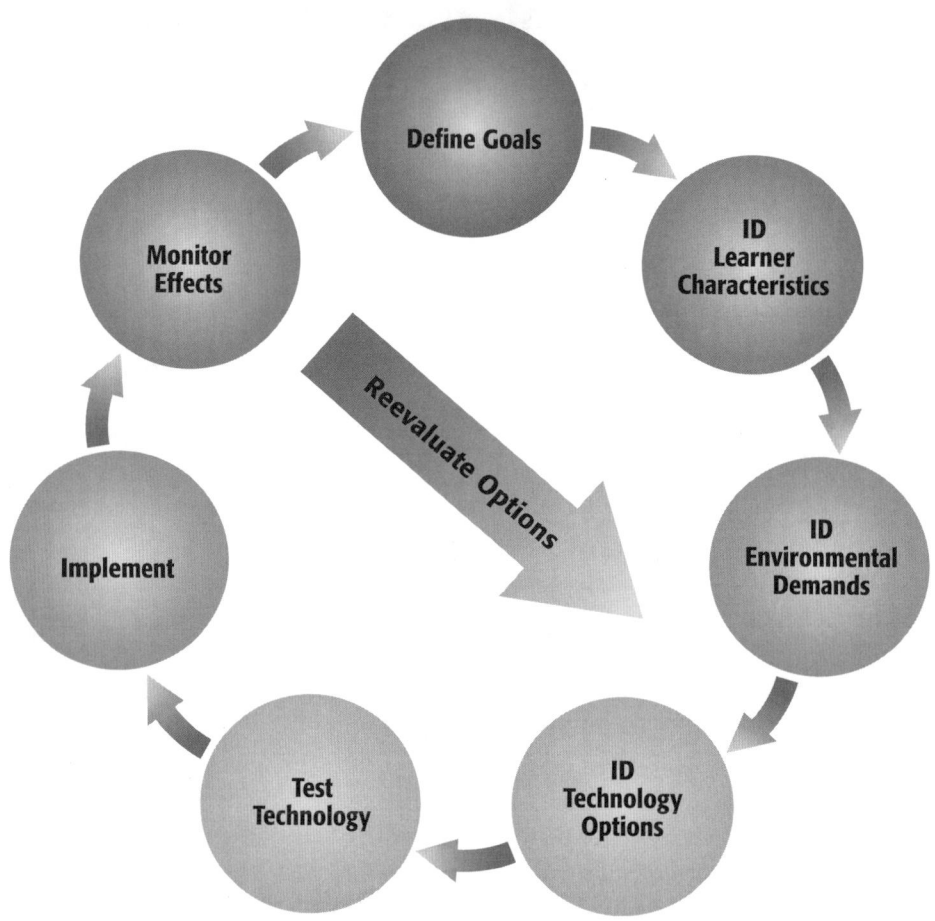

Figure 4.1. The process of selection, implementation, and monitoring. As the figure illustrates, the process is ongoing, recursive, and occasionally in need of reevaluation.

Training

Training learners to use technology typically requires explicit instruction. For instance, teaching a student to use AAC, customizing technology (e.g., preparing a student to use speech-to-text software in a word processor), and orienting students to specific uses of technology (e.g., having students compose work on regular word processors as an AT alternative to writing with paper and pencil) all require instructional time and effort. Furthermore, while students are mastering the technology, teachers need to create naturalistic opportunities to use the technology throughout the learner's schedule. The purpose of this is to provide the learner with ample opportunity to practice using the technology, as well as to ensure that the teacher and student have the technology ready to use (e.g., the AAC device is in close proximity, the laptop is charged).

The process for training the learner to access technology will vary based on the technology demands. Obviously, an important consideration for teachers is to be sure they have had sufficient training to use and teach others to use the technology. One of the legal and policy-related aspects of AT that is frequently overlooked is the AT staff training provision. If teachers do not feel that they have mastery of the technology, then they need to advocate for themselves to get trained. Once a teacher has mastered the technology, he or she needs to structure explicit time to train the student to use the technology.

Some AT (e.g., PECS) comes with explicit training protocols. With others, the training process is largely left up to teachers. Teachers who have to train a learner to use writing software, where many of the processes are chained responses (one step has to be completed before another step can begin), can follow basic task analytic instructional techniques (see Collins, 2012) for examples of task analytic instruction). Likewise, students who are learning to use a calculator to solve arithmetic problems would benefit from systematic response chaining procedures, whereby the teacher prompts them through each step of using the calculator to arrive at the answer. For example, to teach using a calculator, the teacher would begin with a worksheet and a calculator for himself or herself and one for the student. The teacher prompts the first step (looks at the problem) and models looking at (or pointing to) the problem. The teacher would then prompt the following step, to identify the first number of the problem, which he or she might say aloud while pointing at it. Then the teacher would model the second step, pressing the corresponding button on the calculator. After repeating this series multiple times, the teacher would begin to fade the prompting (likely using time delay or least-to-most prompting; see Collins, 2012, for examples).

Assistive Technology

Generally, AT serves a specific support purpose for a learner, such as aiding communication or permitting access to a computer. In mapping out programming, the teacher or lead therapist needs to identify natural opportunities throughout the session, day, or week for the student to use the technology. Students will not achieve the level of independence that AT can provide if they do not have multiple opportunities to learn how to use the technology and sufficient chances to practice with it. Teachers and therapists can facilitate this through careful planning. If a student uses an AAC device to communicate, the teacher and team need to map the student's day to identify all of the areas that might occasion use of this technology and provide appropriate opportunities for instruction. They may have to contrive situations early in the acquisition stage to create more learning opportunities. For example, if the team is working with a 5-year-old child with ASD who is using a nine-button communication device, such as a GoTalk 9+, the team may look at the child's schedule and see that there are three specific contexts in the morning where explicitly focusing on the AAC-related skill would be beneficial. This might be a morning meeting/circle time, taking the attendance report to the office, and a snack period. Each of these contexts may necessitate programming different buttons on the student's device with different messages. Planning this in advance affords the team an opportunity to maximize learning opportunities and ensures that the team members have appropriately programmed the student's AAC.

As a student begins learning how to use AT, the teacher should explicitly arrange opportunities for AT use in such a manner so as to allow sufficient prompting. For example, a student who is in the initial acquisition stages of learning an AAC strategy like PECS will require a second adult to provide prompting and assist with early-stage acquisition. If the student is learning to use a specific piece of software, having another instructor or even a skilled peer available to assist the learner achieve success with the technology will be essential. The number of opportunities across a day or week will vary; however, an IEP or therapy team should use only technologies for which there is a frequent need in that student's life. Therefore, teachers likely won't need to contrive situations for using the technology, but they need to make sure that the student has the technology available at the appropriate times throughout the day and that support for learning to use the tool is available. For students using a calculator to support math, leaving it in their homeroom when they transition to math defeats the purpose of teaching them to use a calculator. Likewise, a student using an AAC device to communicate with adults and peers loses out on important opportunities if the device is left in the classroom when he or she goes to the playground or on community-based instructional trips.

An important consideration with AT relates to the role it serves in supporting a learner. If a child uses AAC to support communication, restricting access to it is akin to taking away his or her voice. If a child uses dictation to write on a computer, not providing an appropriately equipped computer denies the child access to the learning environment. Teachers should always keep in mind that nearly any AT can fail. A student's laptop batteries may lose their charge, a microswitch may get knocked into a sink full of water, and a tablet may get dropped and broken. While teachers (and students) can plan for and avoid some of these challenges with preventive actions, such as plugging in devices to charge batteries or using protective cases, backup systems to support a student should be included in the programming to ensure that the student has continued access to his or her learning environment. This may mean that a student who regularly uses a PECS book (and forgets it) has a backup system at school, such as a laminated card displaying many of his or her most important communication messages. Forethought and planning are required to provide the student with maximally beneficial learning opportunities to achieve AT fluency and use the AT to engage his or her community. Advanced preparation of backup systems will also help to ensure that temporary problems with AT do not impede a student's academic or social progress.

Instructional Technology

Planning for implementation of IT differs somewhat from that of AT. Generally, IT is specifically geared toward supplementing some aspect of teacher-directed instruction. Therefore, planning times for student use of IT will vary with the pace and scheduling of the teacher-led instruction. Teachers should plan to explicitly teach students how to use IT appropriately prior to beginning its formal use. The easiest and most straightforward method for teaching a student to use IT (as well as AT) is to use Behavioral Skills Training (BST; Miltenberger, 2000). BST has been used to teach a wide range of skills and is well suited to teaching a student with ASD to use IT.

There are four basic steps to using BST. First, the teacher provides a brief explanation (1–2 minutes maximum) regarding what the student will do with the technology. Then the teacher models using the technology. Ideally, the teacher will have two technology devices, one he or she can use for modeling and a second one for the student to use. After the teacher models a portion of the software, the next step is to role-play it with the learner. With software, role-playing involves the teacher queueing the software to the point that he or she is teaching and talking the student through each step, that is, as the student does each one. After role-playing, the teacher allows the student an opportunity to use that aspect of the program independently and provides feedback on the student's performance. The teacher repeats this process for all steps or components of the software the student will use.

Planning for student technology use becomes a matter of scheduling once the student has demonstrated he or she can use the software. Generally, for most IT that teachers use to supplement instruction, a student's schedule should be geared for software use. Frequently, depending on the structure of a classroom and the teacher-to-student ratio, teachers can structure IT time during the day for both individual and group work. For instance, teachers may schedule time for some learners to work in small groups with a teacher or aide while other students are scheduled for individualized or independent IT instruction. For a classroom with 10 to 12 students, a teacher, a teaching assistant, and two computers, the teacher can find times to divide students into two small groups of four to five while two students work on the computers.

Where instruction and practice take place during any given day probably has less relevance than when this occurs relative to the student's initial introduction to the material. If a teacher uses IT to help in acquisition and fluency building, the student will likely benefit from some degree of teacher-led instruction first (similar to BST, where practice follows some degree of demonstration and explanation). By carefully evaluating the purpose and potential impact of technology, teachers will learn what technology scheduled at what times will work best for individual students.

Steps of Behavioral Skills Training

1. Explain.
2. Model.
3. Role-play.
4. Provide opportunity for independent practice and feedback.

Monitoring Implementation

As with any teaching method or intervention component, the use of technology and its effects on the student and his or her environment should be monitored on both a short-term and long-term basis. Monitoring implementation of technology serves multiple purposes: ensuring fidelity of implementation, tracking progress (or regression) of the targeted skill or behavior, and tracking potential corresponding behavior changes (e.g., a student using a word processor increases typing speed). For these reasons, teachers need to collect baseline data on the targets, such as progress on a particular academic skill or number of times communication is initiated, before implementing the technology. Having this baseline data will allow teachers and IEP teams to evaluate the effectiveness of the technology and may help guide teams when making decisions about next steps, such as generalization plans and next-step goals and objectives.

One of the most important reasons to monitor implementation of technology, both AT and IT, is to ensure fidelity of implementation. When technology is initially introduced into the environment, the teacher has the responsibility to ensure appropriate use of the technology by both staff and students and to optimize its beneficial effects. Until the student masters the technology, the teacher or paraprofessional will likely have to supervise the student frequently, if not continuously. Creating a task analysis for the technology (see Collins, 2012) may help the teacher ensure procedural fidelity and may also help the student become more independent in utilizing the technology.

Monitoring procedural fidelity should continue even after the student masters the technology and uses it throughout his or her daily schedule. This way, if the student's progress slows, the teacher can compare his or her progress and fidelity data and determine if the slowing progress was a function of a mismatch between the technology and the student's needs or a failure of the staff to follow protocol precisely. As the student progresses and time passes, the teacher may need to modify how and if the student uses technology. By continuing to collect data and monitoring student performance, teachers will have the information they need to justify a change.

A brief discussion of implementing PECS and an iPad communication application exemplifies monitoring implementation to ensure procedural fidelity. When beginning the acquisition process of PECS, the teacher should adhere to the prompting sequence and narration to minimize prompt dependency and establish discrimination of images. Once a student has mastered discrimination of pictures using PECS (i.e., selecting the picture representing the item he or she wants from an array of pictures), the teacher should continue to monitor the use of the PECS book to ensure that the student continues to discriminate between the images and is correctly and functionally using the PECS book. Implementation should continue to be monitored once the student has achieved generalization and fluency with the PECS book. This review process will permit objective and data-based decisions regarding the need and appropriateness for a more advanced device, such as an iPad equipped with a communication application, subsequent to the student's acquisition of basic discrimination skills. As the student transitions to using the iPad as a communication device, the teacher should monitor progress to ensure that the skills learned with PECS generalize to the iPad application (e.g., selecting the image that corresponds with a want or need). Furthermore, the teacher should monitor for appropriate use of the iPad, as the student may be tempted to open other applications. Indeed, teachers may need to put into place security measures or parental control measures.

Monitoring implementation should also encompass keeping data on the student's progress relative to the behavior or skill targeted for technology support. The primary purpose of incorporating technology into a student's daily life is to enhance learning and allow the student to access the instruction. If the technology does not benefit the student's learning, the team should reevaluate the student's use of that particular technology. By monitoring progress and comparing pre- and post-implementation data related to the technology, teachers can determine the impact of the AT or IT on the student's learning. For example, a teacher determined that a student struggling with reading comprehension had a deficit in decoding words, making it challenging for her to complete a reading passage. To support the student in the area of reading comprehension, her teacher began using electronic text that could read the story aloud to her and orally give her comprehension questions and answer choices. Each day during her reading block, the teacher ensured that the student's headphones worked and the volume was correctly set. She then tracked the student's performance while using the program. Before the student started using the electronic text, she regularly failed her reading comprehension tests. However, once the teacher provided the student access and training for the computer program, the student began to correctly respond to comprehension questions. In this scenario, the teacher regularly monitored implementation of the instructional technology by collecting data and looking at the student's performance before and after implementation.

Any time new technology is introduced to an environment, teachers should be aware of potential changes in behavior and make an effort to monitor these changes. As with academic data, data on behavior (e.g., elopement, disruption during work time) should be kept before, during, and after implementation of new technology. Although a change in behavior (e.g., an increase in appropriate classroom behavior, a decrease in undesirable behaviors) may not be the primary purpose of implementing the technology, it is a likely effect of implementing new technology in the classroom. Data on these behaviors may be important in future discussions of the technology related to its continued use or discontinuation.

The purposes of monitoring implementation are as follows:

1. **Ensure procedural fidelity:** Make sure the technology is used when and how it is supposed to be used. Correct application and use should be monitored throughout the student's technology experience, from initial training trials to mastery and beyond. Steps in using the technology should be identified and followed with each use. Certainly, if sequence is important in correctly using the technology, the sequential order should be consistently followed every time.

2. **Ensure appropriate use of the technology:** Advanced technology may allow a student to access games or the Internet (e.g., using an iPad to present discrete trial training [DTT] slides). The student should be monitored for inappropriate use any time the technology is being operated. Barriers such as guided access may need to be put into place to restrict access.

3. **Know when to change technology:** If the technology is not serving its purpose, other options should be explored to pursue learning goals and otherwise maximize student benefits. Depending on the technology, a change may also be warranted if it is successful. For example, consider the case of a student who began using a support for word processing that would read back each individual word as it was typed, and this began to improve the coherence of the student's writing. As the student gained skills and began to compose more fluently, the software could not speak each word quickly enough. In this case, the teacher might set the software to provide the spoken feedback only when the student completed a sentence.

4. **Track the student's progress in the targeted skill (e.g., communication, solving addition problems):** One of the most important jobs of a teacher is to collect data on goals and objectives. Tracking progress on targeted skills enables a teacher to make appropriate decisions on moving to more advanced skills or backing up to prerequisite skills. Data can also be presented to IEP teams to help support decisions for new technology or a change in technology.

5. **Track potentially corresponding behavior changes:** The addition of any new stimulus into an environment can influence a student's behavior. When implementing new technology with a student, teachers should track target behaviors and record data on any new behaviors to support the continuation or change of the current technology for behavior-related reasons.

As the team monitors implementation, team members may find that they need to return to defining their goals. For example, the goals may have been too limited; that is, the expectations were too low and as soon as the student accessed the technology, the student mastered the objectives. In this case, the team needs to identify next steps and how to challenge the student more. Alternatively, the objectives may have been too advanced or unattainable within the time frame. In such instances, the team needs to reconsider either the criterion level, the time parameter, the behaviors specified in the objective, or all three. This may lead the team through reviewing the student characteristics and environmental demands again to evaluate whether these still sufficiently describe the salient contextual variables. The team may find that it does not need to alter the goals for the technology but instead needs to identify other technology options. If this is the case, the team simply reengages the process from that point; works through the identification, testing, and implementation; and continues to monitor student progress.

REVIEW QUESTIONS

1. Why is training in the use of technology for the student, as well as staff and parents, important?
2. What are the key steps in BST?
3. What are the key components of implementation that need to be monitored?

DISCUSSION QUESTIONS

1. What are some strategies or arguments that teachers might be able to use to advocate for technology training for themselves or their students?
2. What rationales might a teacher provide to staff for monitoring technology implementation?

Jack and AAC

Jack's teacher followed the protocols for teaching the first three phases of PECS. For each phase, she strategically placed training sessions throughout Jack's typical schedule so that sessions took place in a naturalistic environment and motivation to make requests was contrived within the schedule. For example, Jack's teacher practiced with Jack every day during snack time. She would present several snack options to him and provide him with whichever snack he requested using his PECS book. In this manner, Jack could get up to 30 trials of practice per day using his PECS book to request each separate bite of his snack. Jack had access to his PECS book across all activities during the school day, and in the beginning his teacher complied with every request she could in order to reinforce Jack's use of his PECS book.

After 7 weeks, Jack was reliably discriminating between the pictures from a field of six to request things he wanted and needed across all activities and environments at his school. Because of his rapid progress with PECS, his proficiency with an iPad, and his newly required discriminating skill, his teacher decided to start the process of transitioning him to a DynaVox device, the electronic speech-generating communication tool preferred by the school's speech–language pathologist (SLP). To begin, the teacher worked with the SLP to set up a DynaVox in a way that reflected Jack's current abilities—images of preferred items and common needs, pages that displayed no more than six images at a time, and a male voice output.

Jack's teacher started incorporating training on the DynaVox into specific times of the day, such as morning calendar, snack time, and independent work. She used a least-prompts method to help him use the DynaVox to respond to academic requests (e.g., counting to 10, stating his name) and to make requests for his wants and needs. Jack's PECS book was available at any time his teacher was not working with him on the DynaVox so that he could continue to communicate his wants and needs.

Jack's teacher also collected and monitored his progress using the Communication Data Sheet shown here. This system allowed his teacher to monitor the level of prompting Jack required to use the DynaVox, what items he requested, and if he produced any vocalizations when he used the device. The teacher also kept track of the locations and communication partners, recording data for Jack's generalization of the device. Blank data sheets can be found in Appendix A for the reader's use.

Communication Data Sheet for Jack (PECS)

Session #	Location, activity	Materials	Communication partner (CP), prompter	Level of prompting	Vocalizations	Problem behavior?
1	Classroom, snack	PECS book, Goldfish, cookies	CP – teacher Prompter – paraprofessional	P	None	None
2	Classroom, snack	PECS book, chips, cookies	CP – teacher Prompter – paraprofessional	P	None	Aggression – 2
3	Classroom, snack	PECS book, Goldfish, grapes	CP – teacher Prompter – paraprofessional	P	None	None
4	Classroom, snack	PECS book, chips, cookies	CP – paraprofessional Prompter – teacher	I	None	None
5	Classroom, snack	PECS book, Goldfish, cookies	CP – paraprofessional Prompter – teacher	I	None	Aggression – 1
6	Classroom, snack	PECS book, grapes	CP – teacher Prompter – paraprofessional	I	None	None
7	Classroom, snack	PECS book, chips, Goldfish	CP – teacher Prompter – paraprofessional	I	None	None
8	Classroom, snack	PECS book, Goldfish, cookies	CP – teacher Prompter – paraprofessional	I	None	None
9	Classroom, snack	PECS book, grapes, Goldfish	CP – teacher Prompter – paraprofessional	I	"guh"	None
10	Classroom, snack	PECS book, chips, cookies	CP – teacher Prompter – paraprofessional	I	None	Aggression – 3

P = Physical   I = Independent (no prompts needed)

Case Study 4.2

Dante's Access to Technology

After acquiring speech-to-text technology, Dante's teacher moved a computer to the corner of her classroom to set up a "writing station" for Dante. The writing station provided Dante some privacy while he worked, while also limiting the amount of background noise that could be picked up by the speech-to-text technology and reducing distractions for the other students. For the next week, the occupational therapist used the class's language arts block to train both Dante and his aide on navigating the speech-to-text technology. The occupational therapist also walked the aide through troubleshooting some common technical problems that could occur with the technology. The teacher posted step-by-step instructions by the computer for both Dante and his aide to reference at any time. Dante's aide saved each day's work to a file so they could track his progress toward the short-term goal of writing a three-paragraph story with no more than two errors in grammar or spelling. To accurately assess Dante's true grammar and spelling abilities, the teacher turned off the spelling and grammar check in the computer's writing application.

Initially, Dante's teacher took data on the number of words recorded during 10-minute blocks to track his writing progress and monitor the implementation of the speech-to-text technology. The teacher provided Dante with familiar writing prompts while he was learning to use the technology and gave him 10 minutes to compose a narrative from those prompts. After 4 days, Dante's word output was comparable to the average of the class, and his teacher decided he was ready to start using the technology to participate in the same writing activities as his peers. He participated in the language arts lessons with the rest of his class. Then, when the class practiced independent writing, Dante went to his writing center and participated in the same writing activities by using the computer and his speech-to-text technology. Dante's aide stayed with him throughout the language arts block to deal with any technology problems, but she no longer helped Dante with his writing assignments.

Typing Data Sheet for Dante—Acquisition

Date	Writing prompt	Words per minute	Total words during session	# of grammar errors	# of spelling errors
9/5/17	If I had a magic carpet, I would . . .	3	30	10	6
9/6/17	If I had a magic carpet, I would . . .	6	58	8	4
9/7/17	If I were president for a day . . .	7	70	8	2
9/8/17	If I were president for a day . . .	8	79	9	5

Sophie Learning From Technology

Sophie's teacher used an iPad to teach Sophie verbs. First the teacher worked to secure Sophie's attention while using the iPad. Following this initial step, the teacher used instructional slides on the iPad every day for a week. In just 5 days, Sophie mastered several of the target verbs. The teacher also noticed that Sophie's problem behaviors during work, such as elopement from the work area or disruption of work materials, decreased in frequency once she began using the iPad for verb instruction.

As shown in the two data sheets for Sophie, the teacher found that using the iPad in conjunction with a systematic prompting strategy, that is, using the moving images to teach expressive identification of verbs, was a successful strategy with Sophie. After 2 weeks of direct instruction, Sophie mastered expressive identification of 25 new verbs. However, she was not reliably identifying verbs during daily activities. To promote generalization, Sophie's teacher decided to incorporate multiple exemplars of each verb into the regular instruction. Additionally, Sophie's teacher began identifying (*tacting*, in the verbal behavior lexicon) the targeted verbs throughout Sophie's natural environment. For example, when Sophie drank her milk at breakfast and lunch, her teacher would comment, "Drinking! You're drinking your milk, Sophie."

Sophie's Still Image Data Sheet

Student: Sophie						Date:	10/19/17				
Target verb	1	2	3	4	5	6	7	8	9	10	% correct
Jumping	P	P	P	P	P						0 (says "shirt")
Eating	I	I	P	P	I						60 (says "?")
Sleeping	I	P	P	P	P						20 (says "pillow")
Drinking	P	P	P	P	P						0 (says "cup")
Writing	P	I	P	P	I						40 (says "pencil")
Coloring	P	P	P	P	P						0 (says the color)
Driving	I	P	P	I	P						40 (says "car")
Walking	P	P	P	P	P						0 (says "shirt" or "boy")
Running	P	P	P	P	P						0 (says "shirt" or "boy")
Swinging	P	I	P	P	I						40 (says "swing")
Sliding	P	P	P	P	P						0 (says "slide")
Laughing	P	I	P	I	P						40 (says "girl")
Sitting	P	P	P	P	P						0 (says "chair")

I = Independent   P = Prompt (verbal prompt is controlling prompt).

Sophie's Moving Image Data Sheet

Student: Sophie						Date:	10/29/17				
Target verb	1	2	3	4	5	6	7	8	9	10	% correct
Jumping	I	I	I	P	I						80
Eating	I	I	I	I	I						100
Sleeping	I	I	I	I	I						100
Drinking	P	I	I	I	I						80
Writing	P	I	I	I	I						80
Coloring	P	P	I	I	I						60
Driving	I	I	I	I	I						100
Walking	I	I	I	I	I						100
Running	I	P	I	I	I						80
Swinging	P	I	P	I	I						60
Sliding	I	I	I	I	I						100
Laughing	P	I	I	I	I						80
Sitting	I	I	I	I	I						100

I = Independent   P = Prompt (verbal prompt is controlling prompt)

Case Study Questions

1. What are some advantages of progressing Jack from PECS to a voice output communication device?
2. What are some challenges the team might have encountered in Jack's case if they had started him with a voice output communication device like a DynaVox rather than first using PECS to prepare him for using a DynaVox device?
3. Why would Dante's teacher consider turning off the spelling and grammar check on the word processor? Could that spelling and grammar check be considered another form of AT for Dante?
4. Sophie's teacher did two things to promote generalization. What were those steps?
5. Even though the teacher focused on teaching Sophie to label verbs in the natural environment (teaching her to *tact*, based on verbal behavior methodology), she needs to consider going at least another step to further increase the likelihood of generalization. What else should the teacher ask of Sophie in the natural environment?

5 Designing Technology Solutions for Discrete Trial Instruction

Since the early days of the Apple IIGS (Apple released HyperCard in 1987), educators have leveraged technology to create their own instructional materials. A common linchpin in much of this development is a tech-savvy teacher (but not a programmer) exploiting commercially packaged software, such as PowerPoint, Keynote, or Slides, to do things that the software was not designed to do. In other words, teachers have taken these platforms and used the components of these software packages, such as authoring tools, to produce educational materials that go beyond generic presentations or lectures. Other, more advanced authoring software packages provide more advanced options, but here we will focus on those tools that are most accessible for teachers.

By creating their own instructional materials, teachers can customize them to directly meet their students' needs and their curriculum. They can incorporate evidence-based practices in a manner that will maximize learning outcomes for their students. This chapter provides educators with step-by-step instructions for using common presentation-type software to build discrete trial types of activities; the next chapter provides an overview of how to develop learning supports for multi-step chained tasks. Readers will learn ways to use evidence-based teaching methods to deliver instruction in one-on-one arrangements as well as small groups.

When students have goals that require discrete responses (e.g., vocabulary words, number identification) teacher-designed technology solutions can provide efficient and effective options. Teachers often rely on free or low-cost Web sites and mobile apps to give students an opportunity to practice these types of academic responses. However, teachers who invest a bit more time into developing customized solutions can provide students with the individualized prompting and error correction that they may need. The following section provides the reader with step-by-step instructions for creating software-run learning materials that use slides (e.g., PowerPoint slides). Depending on the specific software, teachers will have different options. Fundamentally, however, the scope and sequence described in the next section will allow the teacher to create an infinite number of digital flashcards that can be used in one-on-one instruction, in small groups, or even as an independent learning activity. For instruction, the teacher can use typical evidence-based instructional strategies, such as time delay or least-to-most prompting methods (see Collins et al., 2014, for step-by-step instructions on response prompting strategies). The following instructions will also provide suggestions for variations and simplification for use with other prompting methods. In general, a basic understanding of how this design logic works should allow for development of customized materials across a range of topic areas. For purposes of illustration, the steps are described within the context of the following instructional goal: a student receptively matches world capitals to their respective countries. Figure 5.1 shows a sample slide sequence.

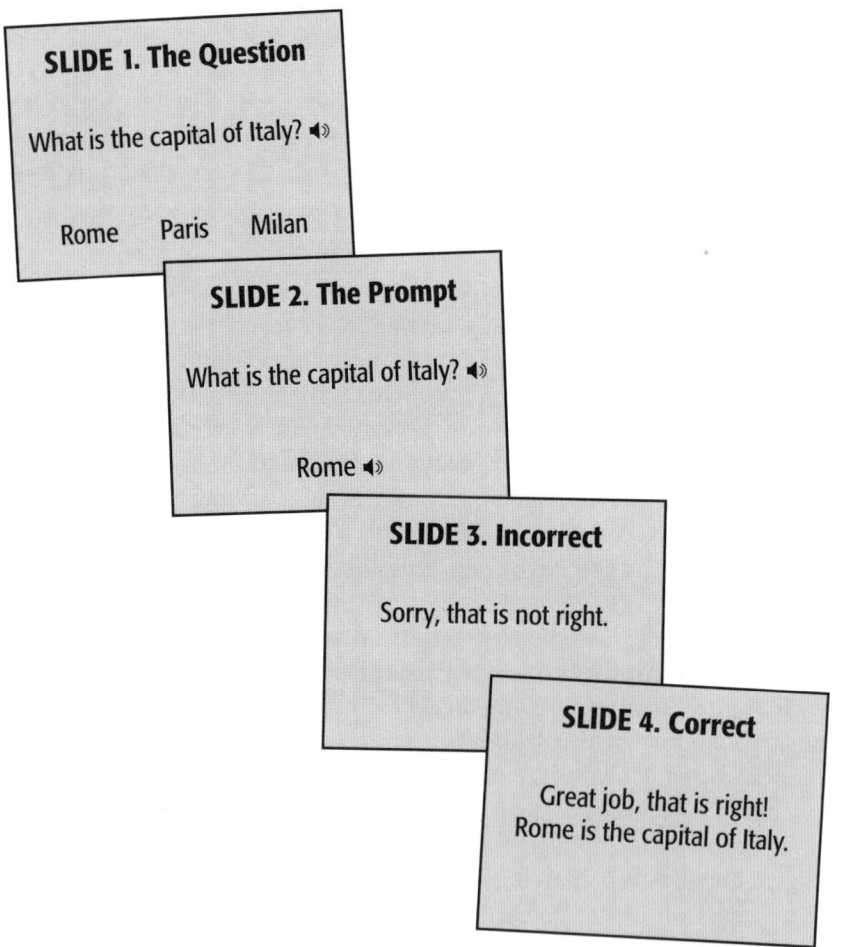

Figure 5.1. Example slide sequence. If the learner selects *Rome* in slide 1, the presentation jumps to slide 4 and continues to the next question. If the learner waits, the presentation jumps to slide 2 to prompt and then returns to slide 1. If the user incorrectly guesses *Paris* or *Milan*, the presentation jumps to slide 3 and then returns to slide 1 to repeat the trial.

Step 1. Create a template for a set of four slides.

As shown in Table 5.1, the purpose of each slide is identified. Additionally, for ease of reference, each slide has a title that can serve as a place holder. Each discrete trial question or stimulus requires this set of four slides. For example, if the student's instructional target is *Rome* (i.e., the answer to the question "What is the capital of Italy?"), the teacher will use four slides. The first slide presents the question, the second provides a prompt, the third offers corrective feedback for an incorrect answer, and the fourth provides reinforcement for a correct response. If the next target is *Paris* (i.e., the answer to the question about the capital of France), the teacher will insert another four slides to build the trial.

Step 2. Manage transitions.

Transitions will vary from presentation package to presentation package. In sum, this step requires the teacher to alter how the presentation software advances from slide to slide. Teachers should keep in mind they are altering the original design of a software when they create individualized instructional materials, and thus some trial-and-error work may be required. The key is that when a finalized stack of instructional slides is complete, the user should not simply be able to proceed in sequence from one to the next. The process would be analogous to a presentation where the speaker displays slides that correspond to particular points and themes rather than shows them in a preestablished sequence. Thus, as related to instructional protocol, slides should be ordered in a fashion that aligns with a learner's responses rather than progressing in a linear sequence.

To achieve this step in PowerPoint, the user needs to highlight all of his or her slides and then locate the option for Transitions. Here, depending on the software version being used, there will be a default option checked for the slides to advance On Mouse Click. At this point, the educator would uncheck the On Mouse Click box. The process is similar in Keynote. After setting up a series of

Table 5.1. Template for a Set of Four Slides

Slide	Title	Purpose
1	Question	Presents the target stimulus or question, along with possible responses
2	Prompt	Provides a prompt after a set period of time
3	Incorrect	Provides error correction and routes the user back to the question slide to try again
4	Correct	Provides reinforcement and directs the user to the next slide

slides, the user navigates to the document preferences and changes the presentation type to Links Only. Each slide will also require further manipulation. With Google Slides, the user does not have the option to override the default transition (which responds to mouse clicks or keyboard arrows). The manipulation here will look similar to what is described for Keynote. In all cases, when the learner uses the software, he or she should rely on the mouse to navigate and not the keyboard. If during the design process these options cannot be found, a fairly simple alternative exists. We will refer to it as the "invisible button." The invisible button involves using the software to draw a transparent box across the entire slide. While it can be colored, this button can be used to cover up the background of the slide so that a mouse click on the slide itself does not advance the slide. Once the button is drawn, the user needs to create a hyperlink by right clicking the mouse, or holding down Ctrl-K (Windows) or Command-K (Mac). This will allow the user to make a link to any slide in the presentation. In this case, the link should be made directly to the slide that is currently being manipulated (i.e., a link to nowhere). At this point, all other transitions to slides will be controlled by timing or user clicks.

Step 3. Save this template set.

To avoid the need to complete the first two steps described above every time a new set is created, the teacher can simply save the newly designed package as a template (e.g., as DiscreteTrialTemplateSlides). Thereafter, the instructor will begin a new file by copying and pasting into the new file as many four-slide sets as there are questions. For example, if the student has 10 vocabulary words, the teacher would copy and paste the set 10 times into the new file (and end up with a total of 40 slides).

Step 4. Setting up slide 1—The question.

On slide 1 the teacher will prepare the question for the student. In our example, we are using countries and capitals. Therefore, if the objective is for the learner to match Italy with its capital, the teacher can write out "What is the capital of Italy?" at the top of the slide. Depending on the reading ability of the student, the teacher can also record narration that mirrors the text. The teacher could, for other learning scenarios, include images or brief videos to augment or support the question. Once the question is set, the teacher needs to provide response options. There are a few ways to do this, depending on the technology skills and comfort level of the teacher or designer. The easiest option is to draw several boxes at the bottom of the screen, with each box representing a different matching option. In our example we might use four boxes. Each box would contain different text (e.g., *Paris,*

Madrid, Berlin, Rome). For each of the first three boxes, the next step is to insert a link (the same as with the invisible button) that goes to the Incorrect slide. When the user selects one of these options, the slide jumps to the Incorrect slide. For the correct response, a link is made to the Correct slide. Given that some learners (with or without ASD) will overselect on irrelevant features such as position or arrangement, returning to the slides periodically to rearrange the order can be beneficial. At this point all of the relevant design features for using the slide in simple trial-and-error learning are finished. If the teacher intends to use this as a self-directed activity, the next step helps with setting up the time delay.

Step 5. Setting up a time delay.

There are three basic options for setting up a time delay when using presentation software of this nature. If the teacher is mediating the delay (i.e., he or she is leading instruction and at least partially operating the software), the easiest solution is to place another invisible button in a corner of the first slide that links to the prompt slide. There are two options if the student will use the slides alone. The first is to set up the first slide to automatically transition to the prompt slide after a set period of time. When following a strict, constant time delay model, the teacher would likely want to create two sets of slides, one with a 0-second delay and one with the delay interval set to 3–5 seconds. Setting the automatic transition varies between PowerPoint and Keynote, but in general requires the designer to start on the slide from which the user will transition and then make a manipulation to the transition again. In PowerPoint, in the same location where the teacher unchecked On Mouse Click to adjust that transition, there should be an option that reads "After" that allows for varying amounts of time. If the teacher wants the slide to transition after 3 seconds of no responding, then he or she sets the number to 3. When the student does not respond for 3 seconds, this setup will advance the slide to the Prompt slide (which is why it was placed second). Similarly in Keynote, where the transitions were altered in the document settings, the designer will use the options for Animate. The user needs to make sure that no images or buttons are currently highlighted by the mouse. Animate will then provide an option to have the slide advance automatically after a set time frame. After the time trigger sends the student to the prompt slide, the teacher has to insert a button on the prompt slide to send the learner back to the question slide.

The other option with both PowerPoint and Keynote is to build animation into the first slide such that it appears only after the delay interval has passed. One advantage of this is that the student does not have to skip between slides. In this case, the teacher would draw another shape or record another audio clip to be used as the prompt. From either the Animations settings in PowerPoint or the Build Out settings in Keynote, the teacher would tell the program when to present the prompt (e.g., 3 seconds after the slide question is read). Different prompts and different instructional arrangements would dictate which strategy the teacher uses in slide design. This arrangement provides the basic structure that permits either teacher-guided or independent student work, depending on learner needs.

Step 6. Setting up feedback.

The slides for correct responses and errors serve two purposes. First, they provide the user with information on the accuracy of his or her response. Second, they direct the flow of the slides to either the next question (if the student responded correctly) or back to the question slide (if the student responded incorrectly). Either way, the simplest way to achieve this navigation is to insert an arrow button on each slide that the teacher instructs the student to use to advance the slides. In the case of the Correct slide, the button should advance the student to the next question. With the Incorrect slide, the button should lead the student back to the question slide to repeat the trial.

Conclusions

These steps should provide teachers with the basic outline for how to structure and customize discrete trial instruction materials. There are many possible variations and manipulations, but these basic instructions should allow teachers a means to develop simple and straightforward materials for individual or group instruction. If teachers plan to use these materials as part of either teacher-led instruction in a one-on-one arrangement or in a small/whole group, they will be able to coach the student(s) through the use of them. On the other hand, if they plan for the student to practice independently, they must first teach the student to use the materials.

The most straightforward way to teach the student is to follow the BST model described previously. First the teacher would explain (briefly) what the student will do with the computer and why. After this brief explanation, the teacher would model the use of the software. The teacher would then assist the student through using the software. Finally, the teacher would provide feedback to the student as he or she tries to use the software independently. Given the instructional setup described here, the teacher will need to continue monitoring the student's engagement and collecting data on his or her performance. Teachers should also consider, as with any discrete trial type of instruction using technology or otherwise, to check for generalization. For example, if a student uses a set of slides designed like those described here to learn basic science vocabulary, then the teacher should evaluate generalization by asking the student questions about that vocabulary orally, having the student respond in a written or alternative format. If the student can respond correctly only in a technology-based lesson, then the instruction was ineffective at achieving meaningful behavioral changes.

REVIEW QUESTIONS

1. In what instructional settings can technology-based discrete trial instruction be used?
2. List three programs that can be used by teachers to design customized discrete trial instruction.
3. Why should a teacher continue to monitor a student's use of technology-based instruction in an independent work setting?

DISCUSSION QUESTIONS

1. What are some rationales that would support teachers creating their own discrete trial instructional materials rather than purchasing pre-packaged software?
2. Why is current technology more suited to teachers building receptive identification types of activities rather than expressive types?
3. What are some things that a teacher might consider doing to increase the likelihood that a student will generalize what he or she has learned from a software-based lesson, like that described here, to similar activities in other contexts?

Case Study 5.1 Jack and AAC Wrap-Up

After 2 weeks, Jack was using his DynaVox throughout the day and across all school settings. When presented with both his DynaVox and his PECS book, Jack consistently selected the DynaVox, a sign to his teacher that this was his preferred mode of communication. As he continued to progress, the school SLP added more images to the device. Jack is now selecting from a field of eight images per page. Although Jack now exclusively uses his DynaVox, his teacher keeps his old PECS book updated with any new images added to the DynaVox and stores it in the classroom closet, in case Jack's DynaVox ever breaks, the batteries run low, or the device malfunctions. The Communication Data Sheet provided here shows Jack's progress using the DynaVox. The teacher used the same data sheet to assess Jack's PECS-program progress.

Communication Data Sheet for Jack (DynaVox)

Session #	Location, activity	Materials	Communication partner (CP), prompter	Level of prompting	Vocalizations	Problem behavior?
1 (2/5/18)	Classroom, snack	DynaVox, chips	CP – paraprofessional	I	None	None
2	Workstation, classroom	DynaVox, marker	CP – teacher	I	None	None
3	Recess	DynaVox, swing	CP – paraprofessional	I	None	None
4	Workstation, classroom	DynaVox, Skittles	CP – paraprofessional	I	None	None
5	Lunch	DynaVox, juice, ketchup	CP – teacher	I	None	None
6 (2/6/18)	Classroom, snack	DynaVox, grapes	CP – teacher	I	"guh"	None
7	Workstation, classroom	DynaVox, marker, M&Ms	CP – paraprofessional	I	None	None
8	Recess	DynaVox, chase	CP – teacher	I	None	None
9	Workstation, classroom	DynaVox, work materials	CP – paraprofessional	I	None	None
10	Lunch	DynaVox, fork	CP – teacher	I	None	None

I = Independent (no prompts needed)

50

Dante and Accessing Tech Wrap-Up

After 3 months of using the speech-to-text technology to complete writing assignments, Dante met his goal to compose a three-paragraph story with no more than two errors in grammar or spelling. In fact, Dante typically composes writing assignments with no grammatical or spelling errors and is so fluent with the technology that he writes two-page stories during the writing block. Dante has expressed his happiness with the technology, and his aide reports that Dante is proud of his independence in writing his narratives. At the next team meeting, Dante's teacher plans to propose incorporating the speech-to-text technology into different academic blocks throughout the day, such as social studies and science.

Accessing Tech Data Sheet for Dante (Typing Data Sheet—Fluency)

Date	Writing prompt	Words per minute	Total words during session	# of grammar errors	# of spelling errors
12/12/17	You have just discovered a secret time machine! Write a story about your adventure to the past.	7	68	6	5
12/15/17	When you went to feed your dog this morning, he started talking! Describe your day with your dog.	8	81	3	2
12/19/17	One morning I got to school and discovered my pencil was magical! What happened that day?	8	80	1	2
1/3/18	You have just been given your dream job! What do you do? Describe one day in your dream job.	9	90	1	1

Sophie Learning With Tech Wrap-Up

Over the next several weeks, Sophie's teacher continued to target verbs, using PowerPoint slides, multiple exemplars, prompting strategies, and generalization methods. Sophie began to spontaneously and correctly use the verbs in multiple school settings. Sophie's parents reported an increase in her use of language at home as well. As Sophie continued to master this skill, her teacher began incorporating programs for eliciting more elaborate responses, extending the target responses to include nouns and adjectives. For example, instead of the basic and original response "brush," the target response expectation became "brushing her hair." By including related words in the target response, Sophie's teacher hoped to continue to expand her vocabulary and shape her generalization skills to include multiple environments.

Questions

1. What are some next steps Jack's teacher could take to continue supporting his AT use?
2. Now that Jack can consistently use his AAC device to make requests across multiple settings, what are two new possible short-term goals for Jack that incorporate his DynaVox?
3. How could Dante's teacher continue to incorporate speech-to-text technology across Dante's school day?
4. Why should the technology team consider a student's opinion on the AT or IT he or she uses?
5. How could Sophie's teacher adapt PowerPoint to teach other skills?

6 Designing Instruction for Multi-Step Skills

Teacher-designed technology for instructing multi-step skills can take several forms. Most of the research in this area has involved evaluations of various types of video-based instruction (prompting or modeling; see Mechling, 2005; Prater, Carter, Hitchcock, & Dowrick, 2012; and Shukla-Mehta, Miller, & Callahan, 2010, for reviews). Notwithstanding the use of videos in this research, teachers can substitute pictures or photographs for video if the student does not require that level of support. In fact, some learners may require or learn best when supported via still stimuli and images rather than the fleeting images of video. If a student fails to attend during critical moments in the video, the student may not see what he or she needs to see and fail to benefit from the prompt. In contrast, still images only necessitate that a student briefly glance at them, if the image displays sufficient information, and the student's attention does not have to occur at a specific point in time. On the other hand, still images obviously do not show the student the topography and other real-life features of the desired response. If the teacher has concerns about whether a student will attend the entire time, shorter videos paired with still photos may help.

When using videos, teachers are encouraged to make video recordings on mobile devices and present them to students. This can be done either as a model (viewing the entire video before doing the task) or as a prompt (showing the video at the point at which the student needs extra assistance). Teachers may want to use video as a component of instruction for multi-step tasks for several reasons. First, if teachers are teaching a skill and they have only a single set of materials (e.g., one microwave), they would not want to model a step and then undo what they just did to provide the learner a chance to do it. This could result in the learner imitating the step completion process as well as the undoing of the step. Second, video-based supports ensure that the learner consistently sees the same model every time.

In general, researchers have reported that video prompting tends to result in faster acquisition with fewer errors than video modeling (Cannella-Malone et al., 2006; Cannella-Malone et al., 2011). With video modeling, learners see an entire sequence and must remember what they saw versus seeing only those parts of the task they need, as is the case with video prompting. Video modeling arguably requires little more than filming a video and showing it to a student. For that reason this section focuses on video prompting.

Teachers can purchase a few all-purpose applications for using video-based instruction. However, they can just as easily design their own applications and exploit some common free applications to implement video prompting. To use video prompting, a teacher could shoot a video and try to jump to the points in the video where he or she needs to deliver a prompt and provide instruction. This may result in slowed instruction and challenges in timing. One way teachers can address this is by editing the video into smaller clips and embedding them either in a playlist in a media player app on a mobile device or inserting them into presentation software, such as PowerPoint, Slides, and KeyNote.

Teachers need to consider storage space when using video on mobile devices. One alternative to storing a lot of video on a device is to store it in the cloud and allow the device to show the remotely stored video. Google Slides provides one of the easiest ways to do this. The downside to this approach is the amount of data that has to be transmitted via WiFi or cellular signal. The following sections provide a general outline for creating materials that teachers can use to lead instruction or that they can turn over to the student to use in a self-instructional format.

Step 1. Task analyze the skill.

The teacher can either shoot the video first or write the steps out first. Either way, the teacher needs to explicitly decide on the sequence of steps to be taught. Many chained responses do not require someone to follow in lockstep (e.g., when making a sandwich, one can usually add the lettuce, meat, or cheese in any order), but some do (e.g., dialing a phone number). Deciding on a single sequence, however, will simplify instruction and provide for more consistent teaching.

Step 2. Shoot the video.

When beginning to shoot the video model, teachers have several decisions to make—who will be in the video, should they narrate the video, point of view, and so forth. Social learning theory research (Bandura, 1969) suggests that a model who looks like the learner generates the most imitation (i.e., if the teacher is working with a young boy with ASD, another young boy would make a good model), albeit some researchers have had success using very different models. In one comparison study (Jones & Schwartz, 2004), the researchers compared three types of models: an adult, a peer, and a sibling. While participants learned under all three models, none resulted in significantly faster acquisition than the others. Getting a peer to serve as a model may serve as a beneficial similarity variable.

In some instances, depending on the skill being taught, the teacher can shoot the video from a point-of-view perspective. For example, a video on hand washing would show only the model's hands. For social skills, however, the teacher should consider including all aspects of the model that are critical to the skill (e.g., facial expressions linked to teaching a greeting skill). Another option for a model would be the learner himself or herself. For this option, called video self-modeling (for reviews, see Buggey, 1995, and Mason, Davis, Ayres, Davis, & Mason, 2016), the teacher would prompt the student through the entire response sequence while filming him or her. Then the teacher would edit out all of the prompts from the video so the student appeared to independently perform the task without error.

Regardless of whom teachers use as a model, they may want to take slightly longer pauses after each step to facilitate editing and to highlight what the environment should look like after completion of a step. They can also do this while editing. When shooting the video, teachers may opt to narrate the steps as they do them or add narration when they edit. Work by Smith, Ayres, Mechling, and Smith (2013) suggests that narration may assist some students in skill acquisition. Further, it may provide an opportunity for incidental learning of language associated with the skill.

Step 3. Edit the video.

The manner in which a teacher cuts a video into clips will vary depending on the mechanics of the editing software he or she uses. The end goal is to have 5- to 10-second clips that show the entirety of a step. Naming each clip with the step number and a few words about the step will facilitate sequencing the steps later. If using Slides, the teacher will need to upload these clips to YouTube. Uploading video with human actors to any server always raises privacy issues, and thus teachers need to consult with their school district regarding these policies. Although YouTube allows users to list clips as private, teachers should still proceed cautiously.

Step 4. Build the presentation package.

At this stage the teacher has the raw materials to create a video prompting sequence. The presentation software can be set up in a few different ways. One way is to display all the videos on a single slide. To do this, the teacher would size the videos so that the thumbnails take up only a small portion of the slide and then change the video formatting so that the video plays on the full screen. This set up permits quick access to any clip, as needed. If using the Google Slides/YouTube method, this will not work. For the latter, the teacher can place each clip on a separate slide and then navigate to that slide when needed, or he or she can include buttons (similar to those discussed in creating discrete trial materials) that permit navigation to individual slides as needed.

Important Considerations Before Shooting

- Perspective of the video: From what perspective should the video be recorded?
- Model in the video: Who should perform the steps in the recording?
- Setting of the video: What should be the setting in which the video is shot and the targeted skill modeled?
- Steps depicted in the video: What steps must the student perform to successfully complete the task?

Teacher-Led Instruction

In teacher-led instruction, teachers have a few options for how they use what they have created. Research supporting both video modeling and video prompting suggests that teachers should provide the student with a preview of the entire sequence of responses (i.e., watch the video uninterrupted) before asking the student to do the task. In some instances they can omit this step, especially if the student has had past experience with the activity, and begin using video as a prompt in either a time-delay arrangement or a least-to-most prompt sequence. Time delay was discussed earlier, and the reader can find more detail in dedicated methods texts (e.g., Collins et al., 2014). If the teacher plans to use the video in accordance with a least-to-most procedure, then the video can take the place of a model prompt in the hierarchy. A three-step least-to-most hierarchy might begin with a verbal prompt, progress to the video prompt, and conclude with physical guidance. After establishing a prompt hierarchy, the teacher then identifies a latency parameter (how long he or she will allow the student to independently initiate a step of the chain before delivering a prompt) and a duration parameter (how long he or she will allow a student to complete a step). If the student does not respond within that latency parameter or begins to make an error, the teacher interrupts the student and delivers the next prompt in the hierarchy. Likewise, if the student exceeds the duration parameter, the teacher interrupts and provides the next level of prompting. This continues through the entire sequence of steps.

Self-Instruction

In a self-instructional arrangement, the learner uses the technology much like an AT type of support. If using a sequence of video prompts like the ones outlined above, the student can refer to the video as needed to complete the task. Technology underlies much of the emerging literature on self-instruction and independent learning opportunities (Smith, Shepley, Alexander, & Ayres, 2015). To effectively use self-instruction with video prompting, the teacher needs to first teach the student to use the technology in this manner. Some might be concerned that the student would become overly reliant on the technology. Notwithstanding this concern, and as mentioned earlier, frequently a student fades the use of the technology as he or she becomes more proficient and can perform the response faster without the technology. In many ways this is like using a cookbook to guide task completion; that is, after having used the same recipe over and over, the cook refers to the cookbook only when needed.

Before expecting a student to learn from the technology, the teacher must provide instruction on how to use the technology to self-instruct. A BST model provides a good context for instruction here as well (i.e., explain, model, role-play, and provide feedback). The teacher may need to select several tasks to use as training tasks until the student independently begins to use the IT. For a new learner, teaching the student to take time to look at the video for each step will help to ensure he or she sees the entire response chain. In the long term, teaching a student to use technology in this way can serve as an introductory step to searching out his or her own support resources. For example, a student who learns to self-instruct using materials like those described here can later learn to use YouTube or other online resources to search for and identify video supports to assist with doing other tasks that he or she has an interest in learning.

Important Considerations Before Teaching

- Presentation: What mode will the student use to view the video?
- Prerequisite skills: Will the student need direct instruction on using the selected technology?
- Technology instruction: If needed, how will the student be taught to use the technology?
- Skill instruction: In what instructional setting will the student be expected to use the technology to learn the skill?

Conclusion

These basic steps provide the foundation for teachers to create their own materials to supplement other forms of instruction. Furthermore, consistently and explicitly teaching students to self-manage the materials may lead them to learn to teach themselves. Spending time experimenting (and collecting data) will help teachers form new and better ways to meet the needs of their students with technology. As new technologies emerge and the current technologies evolve, teachers will have new opportunities to engage their students with technology.

In a parallel fashion to preparing for discrete trial instruction, teachers can design custom technology tools for teaching individualized and tailored multi-step chained tasks. In contrast to commercial products, customized strategies permit the use of custom-built images, sounds, video, and so forth. As students progress or their needs change, teachers can adjust what they have designed to the extent the software allows. Furthermore, they can create materials that reflect their local community and recycle these for use with other students. The key for success, regardless of what teachers use or design, revolves around data collection and teacher responsivity to those data.

REVIEW QUESTIONS

1. What are the advantages and disadvantages of using still images to teach multi-step skills? Of using video?
2. Which of the video-based methods is reported to result in faster acquisition and fewer errors? Why?
3. What are some important issues to consider when designing a video for instructional use?

DISCUSSION QUESTIONS

1. Pick a skill that could be taught using video prompting. How might you task analyze this skill? What settings and models would you use to record the video, and why?
2. How would mastering self-instruction through video modeling and video prompting benefit a student in the future?

Jack and Chained Tasks

Jack's teacher was elated with the success of his DynaVox program. Several months after implementation of the program, Jack was more independent and academically successful, and he was using his DynaVox device across multiple school environments. After Jack became fluent in navigating the device and using it independently, his teacher decided to try other forms of technology to further increase his independence in other facets of his life. His IEP team met, and they determined that using video prompting to teach Jack how to do simple classroom tasks, such as unpacking in the morning and returning the snack basket to the cafeteria, would increase his independence in the classroom. His teacher was also excited about the opportunity for Jack to learn self-instruction and the doors it could open for Jack in the future. The team's short-term goal for Jack was as follows: Within 1 month, Jack will independently use video prompting to complete a daily classroom task with 100% accuracy.

Jack's IEP team decided to use video prompting rather than video modeling because of Jack's age and attention span. They determined that Jack would not be able to attend to a whole video before performing a task and that shorter pieces of video highlighting most-current instructional steps would be more appropriate. Before shooting the video, Jack's teacher needed to consider several variables: the setting of the video, the model in the video, the perspective of the video, and the steps shown in the video to successfully complete the task. She filmed the steps in the natural setting in which they should occur (Jack's classroom), using his book bag, school materials, and hook. She also asked a peer who had already mastered the skill to serve as the model for the video. The instructional stimuli were already known and significant to Jack, and the teacher thought they could be used in video form to promote generalization from the video to the target environment. She also decided that a third-person perspective (that is, filming so that viewers could see the entire model and surrounding environment) would also be appropriate for Jack and would likely promote future generalization. After watching the peer model perform the task several times, the teacher wrote out the following steps: (1) Walk to the area of the classroom with the hooks and cubbies. (2) Remove book bag and jacket. (3) Hang up jacket (if applicable). (4) Hang up book bag. (5) Unzip book bag. (6) Remove daily folder. (7) Place folder in the basket with Jack's name on it. (8) Zip book bag. (9) Check visual schedule for the next activity.

Using this information, the teacher filmed the student model performing these specific tasks and edited the video to include a voiceover that verbally directed Jack on what to do for each step as he watched the student model perform it. The teacher set up the videos on the classroom iPad. She chose the iPad because of its similarity in size and use to Jack's DynaVox. For several days, the teacher used BST (previously described) to teach Jack how to manipulate the videos and follow the directions they provided, including pausing a video as he performed the various steps. Jack acquired the self-instruction skills quickly, likely due to the similarity of the iPad to his DynaVox, with which he had been so successful.

Over the next 2 weeks, Jack's teacher instructed him to use the video prompting program each morning to perform the target task of unpacking his book bag. She regularly monitored the implementation of the self-instruction program and collected data on whether he performed each step independently and if he used the technology appropriately and independently.

 Case Study ## Questions

1. What is another classroom task that Jack's teacher could use self-instruction through video prompting to teach? Write a task analysis for that skill.
2. How can Jack benefit from mastering video-based self-instruction in the future?
3. How could Jack generalize self-instruction to environments other than his school? Brainstorm three other skills Jack could learn through video-based self-instruction in these environments.

7 Summary and Conclusions

Teachers can capitalize on technology to enhance the learning environment and help their students more effectively communicate, access academic content, and achieve their learning objectives. Teachers can also use technology to waste students' time and mask poor instruction. To be sure, technology is not a panacea and will prove beneficial only when correctly applied. Only through matching the technology to learner needs, thoughtful implementation, careful monitoring, and making data-based decisions can teachers fully maximize the potential technology offers.

Part of learning how to use technology to support instruction for individuals with ASD involves learning the process of selection, training, and monitoring. This process entails deciding when and what technology to use and then implementing its use in a deliberate and thoughtful manner. Early in this book, we focused on using a team-based approach that included the student, parents/caregivers, teachers, speech therapists, occupational therapists, and AT specialists to help identify appropriate technology. The identification involved examining the demands of the environment with respect to the current skills and/or functioning of the student and in relation to his or her goals. From here the team can focus their efforts on identifying potential solutions. During this selection process, the team needs to listen to the opinions and preferences of the learner. This may involve dedicating time to allow the student to practice using the technology and determine if it fits his or her needs and how he or she feels about it. For students who cannot communicate vocally, the team should observe their interactions with the technology and attempt to judge their level of receptiveness.

After the team has identified a satisfactory technology solution (i.e., AT or IT) or the teacher has designed appropriate IT materials, the student needs an opportunity to learn how to use the technology. In some cases this may be an informal process of trial and error for the student. In other cases the student may not need any explicit training. Then again, with technology that the student has never previously used, the team should set aside time for training. Putting a student in front of a word processor with word-prediction software without teaching the student how to best use the software will likely result in unsatisfactory outcomes. If the team does not train the student to use the technology (AT or IT) and the student fails to achieve his or her objectives, the team cannot blame the technology. Once the student has mastered use of the technology and implementation begins, the teacher or therapist must then monitor implementation.

Implementation monitoring requires the teacher to track two separate but related things. First, tracking and evaluating student performance with the technology is obviously essential. Second, the teacher has to monitor implementation fidelity. By monitoring implementation fidelity in tandem with student performance, the teacher or therapist is positioned to problem solve treatment failures and intervention adjustments. For example, a team that decides to adopt a tablet-based AAC solution for a student would not want to conclude that it made a poor decision if the student progresses more slowly than anticipated as a result of the staff not making the tablet available across all settings.

These same monitoring factors are important for evaluating teacher-designed IT as well. Keeping track of student performance will help the teacher decide when to add more material or, for example, adjust the prompting protocol. But the teacher also has to monitor how the technology is used. If a paraprofessional leads instruction and does not follow the protocol to use time delay, this may impede learning. Likewise, a student engaged with IT in an independent learning time who instead watches videos on YouTube will not make adequate progress with the materials the teacher created.

Regardless of the technology (tablets or vintage textbooks), children with ASD deserve tools that will enhance their education. The team of teachers, therapists, and other professionals around a student need to make conscious decisions to maximize instructional efficiency. Regardless of what technological breakthroughs enter education, if a student's educational team remains focused on matching technology to the demands of the environment and needs of the learner with a clear focus on measurable outcomes, the team will help the student achieve success. Innovation will continue to provide new mechanisms of support and instruction. Clear, careful consideration of the educational process and evidence-based (analog) practices will help educators avoid being blinded by the glitz of shiny new technologies.

In 1964, Ogden Lindsley discussed the challenges faced by individuals with disabilities and how contemporary environments are ill-suited to meet their needs. In fact, he emphasized that in many ways the obstacles they face in day-to-day life and in learning are as much a function of science's inability to construct appropriate environments as the disabilities themselves. As science advances technology and as individuals with ASD come to both influence innovation and capitalize on that innovation, learning environments and communities will be better able to accommodate their needs. In accommodating their needs, the communities will benefit from the skills and insights these individuals have to offer. Both AT and IT serve as prosthetics that permit a better fit between a person's needs and the demands of the environment. Technological advances will continue to serve to close this gap.

⚙ References

Ayres, K. M., & Cihak, D. (2010). Computer- and video-based instruction of food-preparation skills: Acquisition, generalization, and maintenance. *Intellectual and Developmental Disabilities, 48*(3), 195–208.

Ayres, K. M., & Langone, J. (2002). Acquisition and generalization of purchasing skills using a video enhanced computer-based instructional program. *Journal of Special Education Technology, 17*(4), 15–28.

Ayres, K. M., Langone, J., Boon, R. T., & Norman, A. (2006). Computer-based instruction for purchasing skills. *Education and Training in Developmental Disabilities, 41*(3), 253–263.

Ayres, K. M., Mechling, L., & Sansoti, F. J. (2013). The use of mobile technologies to assist with life skills/independence of students with moderate/severe intellectual disability and/or autism spectrum disorders: Considerations for the future of school psychology. *Psychology in the Schools, 50*(3), 259–271.

Ayres, K. M., Shepley, S. B., Douglas, K. H., Shepley, C., & Lane, J. D. (2016). Mobile technology as a prosthesis: Using mobile technology to support community engagement and independence. In *Technology and the treatment of children with autism spectrum disorder* (pp. 131–145). New York, NY: Springer.

Bandura, A. (1969). *Principles of behavior modification.* New York, NY: Holt, Rinehart and Winston.

Bondy, A. S., & Frost, L. A. (1994). The picture exchange communication system. *Focus on Autistic Behavior, 9*(3), 1–19.

Bouck, E. C., Satsangi, R., Doughty, T. T., & Courtney, W. T. (2014). Virtual and concrete manipulatives: A comparison of approaches for solving mathematics problems for students with autism spectrum disorder. *Journal of Autism and Developmental Disorders, 44*, 180–193.

Buggey, T. (1995). An examination of the effectiveness of videotaped self-modeling in teaching specific linguistic structures to preschoolers. *Topics in Early Childhood Special Education, 15*(4), 434–458.

Cannella-Malone, H. I., Fleming, C., Chung, Y. C., Wheeler, G. M., Basbagill, A. R., & Singh, A. H. (2011). Teaching daily living skills to seven individuals with severe intellectual disabilities: A comparison of video prompting to video modeling. *Journal of Positive Behavior Interventions, 13*(3), 144–153.

Cannella-Malone, H., Sigafoos, J., O'Reilly, M., de la Cruz, B., Edrisinha, C., & Lancioni, G. E. (2006). Comparing video prompting to video modeling for teaching daily living skills to six adults with developmental disabilities. *Education and Training in Developmental Disabilities, 13*(3), 344–356.

Charlop-Christy, M. H., Le, L., & Freeman, K. A. (2000). A comparison of video modeling with in vivo modeling for teaching children with autism. *Journal of Autism and Developmental Disorders, 30*(6), 537–552.

Chen, S. A., & Bernard-Opitz, V. (1993). Comparison of personal and computer-assisted instruction for children with autism. *Mental Retardation, 31*, 368–376.

Coleman-Martin, M. B., Heller, K. W., Cihak, D. F., & Irvine, K. L. (2005). Using computer-assisted instruction and the nonverbal reading approach to teach word identification. *Focus on Autism and Other Developmental Disabilities, 20*(2), 80–90.

Collins, B.C. (2012). *Systematic instruction for students with moderate and severe disabilities*. Baltimore, MD: Brookes Publishing.

Collins, J. C., Ryan, J. B., Katsiyannis, A., Yell, M., & Barrett, D. E. (2014). Use of portable electronic assistive technology to improve independent job performance of young adults with intellectual disability. *Journal of Special Education Technology, 29*(3), 15–29.

Desai, T., Chow, K., Mumford, L., Hotze, F., & Chau, T. (2014). Implementing an iPad-based alternative communication device for a student with cerebral palsy and autism in the classroom via an access technology delivery protocol. *Computers and Education, 79*, 148–158.

DT Trainer [Computer software]. Columbia, SC: Accelerations Educational Software

Fager, S., Hux, K., Beukelman, D. R., & Karantounis, R. (2006). Augmentative and alternative communication use and acceptance by adults with traumatic brain injury. *Augmentative and Alternative Communication, 22*, 37–47.

Higgins, K., & Boone, R. (1996). Creating individualized computer assisted instruction for students with autism using multimedia authoring software. *Focus on Autism and Other Developmental Disabilities, 11*, 69–78.

Hutcherson, K., Langone, J., Ayres, K., & Clees, T. (2004). Computer assisted instruction to teach item selection in grocery stores: An assessment of acquisition and generalization. *Journal of Special Education Technology, 19*(4), 33–42.

Individuals With Disabilities Education Act of 1990, 20 U.S.C. § 1400 *et seq.* (1990).

Jones, C. D., & Schwartz, I. S. (2004). Siblings, peers, and adults: Differential effects of models for children with autism. *Topics in Early Childhood Special Education, 24*(4), 187–198.

Kientz, J. A., Goodwin, M. S., Hayes, G. R., & Abowd, G. D. (2013). Interactive technologies for autism: Synthesis lectures on assistive, rehabilitative, and health-preserving technologies. Toronto, Canada: Morgan & Claypool.

Lindsley, O. (1964). Direct measurement and prosthesis of retarded behavior. *Journal of Education, 147*, 62–81.

Lovaas, I. O. (2003). Teaching individuals with developmental delays: Basic intervention techniques. Austin, TX: PRO-ED.

MacSuga-Gage, A. S., & Simonsen, B. (2015). Examining the effects of teacher-directed opportunities to respond on student outcomes: A systematic review of the literature. *Education and Treatment of Children, 38*, 211–239.

Mason, R. A., Davis, H. S., Ayres, K. M., Davis, J. L., & Mason, B. A. (2016). Video self-modeling for individuals with disabilities: A best-evidence, single case meta-analysis. *Journal of Developmental and Physical Disabilities, 28*(4), 623–642.

McCleery, J. P. (2015). Comment on technology-based intervention research for individuals on the autism spectrum. *Journal of Autism and Developmental Disorders, 45*, 3382–3835.

McKissick, B. R., Spooner, F., Wood, C. L., & Diegelmann, K. M. (2013). Effects of computer-assisted explicit instruction on map-reading skills for students with autism. *Research in Autism Spectrum Disorders, 7*, 1653–1662.

Mechling, L. (2005). The effect of instructor-created video programs to teach students with disabilities: A literature review. *Journal of Special Education Technology, 20*(2), 25–36.

Mechling, L. C., Ayres, K. M., Foster, A. L., & Bryant, K. J. (2013). Comparing the effects of commercially available and custom-made video prompting for teaching cooking skills to high school students with autism. *Remedial and Special Education, 34*(6), 371–383.

Mechling, L. C., Gast, D. L., & Langone, J. (2002). Computer-based video instruction to teach persons with moderate intellectual disabilities to read grocery aisle signs and locate items. *Journal of Special Education, 35*, 224–240.

Miltenberger, R. (2000). Behavioral skills training to remediate deviant social behavior of an adolescent in residential treatment. *Cognitive and Behavioral Practice, 7*, 236–238.

Parette, P., & Scherer, M. (2004). Assistive technology use and stigma. *Education and Training in Developmental Disabilities, 39*(3), 217–226.

Pennington, R. C. (2010). Computer-assisted instruction for teaching academic skills to students with autism spectrum disorder: A review of literature. *Focus on Autism and Other Developmental Disabilities, 25*(4), 239–248.

Prater, M. A., Carter, N., Hitchcock, C., & Dowrick, P. (2012). Video self-modeling to improve academic performance: A literature review. *Psychology in the Schools, 49*(1), 71–81.

Schnorr, C. I., Freeman-Green, S., & Test, D. W. (2016). Response cards as a strategy for increasing opportunities to respond: An examination of the evidence. *Remedial and Special Education, 37*, 41–54.

Shukla-Mehta, S., Miller, T., & Callahan, K. J. (2010). Evaluating the effectiveness of video instruction on social and communication skills training for children with autism spectrum disorders: A review of the literature. *Focus on Autism and Other Developmental Disabilities, 25*(1), 23–36.

Sigafoos, J., O'Reilly, M., Cannella, H., Edrisinha, C., de la Cruz, B., Upadhyaya, M., . . . Young, D. (2007). Evaluation of a video prompting and fading procedure for teaching dish washing skills to adults with developmental disabilities. *Journal of Behavioral Education, 16*(2), 93–109.

Simpson, A., Langone, J., & Ayres, K. M. (2004). Embedded video and computer based instruction to improve social skills for students with autism. *Education and Training in Developmental Disabilities, 39*, 240–252.

Smith, K. A., Ayres, K. M., Alexander, J. A., Ledford, J., Shepley, C., & Shepley, S. (2016). Initiation and generalization of self-instructional skills in adolescents with autism and intellectual disability. *Journal of Autism and other Developmental Disabilities, 46*, 1196–1209.

Smith, K. A., Shepley, S. B., Alexander, J. L., & Ayres, K. M. (2015). The independent use of self-instructions for the acquisition of untrained multi-step tasks for individuals with an intellectual disability: A review of the literature. *Research in Developmental Disabilities, 40*, 19–30.

Smith, M., Ayres, K., Mechling, L., & Smith, K. (2013). Comparison of the effects of video modeling with narration vs. video modeling on the functional skill acquisition of adolescents with autism. *Education and Training in Autism and Developmental Disabilities*, 164–178.

Technology Related Assistance for Individuals with Disabilities Act of 1988, 1 U.S.C. § 2201–2217 (1988).

Travers, J. C., Higgins, K., Pierce, T., Boone, R., Miller, S., & Tandy, R. (2011). Emergent literacy skills of preschool students with autism: A comparison of teacher-led and computer assisted instruction. *Education and Training in Autism and Developmental Disabilities, 46*, 326–338.

Watts, E. H., O'Brian, M., & Wojcik, B. W. (2004). Four models of assistive technology consideration: How do they compare to recommended educational assessment practices? *Journal of Special Education Technology, 19*(1), 43–56.

Zabala, J. S. (1995). *The SETT framework: Critical areas to consider when making informed assistive technology decisions.* Houston, TX: Region IV Education Service Center. (ERIC Document Reproduction Service No. ED 381962)

Appendix A

Blank Data Sheets for Case Studies

AAC Case Study Data Sheet: Communication Data Sheet

Session #	Location, activity	Materials	Communication partner (CP), prompter	Level of prompting	Vocalizations	Problem behavior?

I = Independent (no prompts needed)   G = Gesture   M = Model   V = Verbal   P = Physical

Accessing Tech Case Study Data Sheet: Typing Data Sheet

Date	Writing prompt	Words per minute	Total words during session	# of grammar errors	# of spelling errors

DTT Verbs Data Sheet (Sophie's Case Study)

Student:							Date:				
Target verb	1	2	3	4	5	6	7	8	9	10	% correct

I = Independent   P = Prompt (verbal prompt is controlling prompt)

Chained-Task Case Study Data Sheets

Student:		Target skill:							
Steps:	Date:								
% Correct:									

I – Independent   VP – Video Prompt

About the Editor and Authors

Richard L. Simpson is professor emeritus, University of Kansas. During his more than 40 years as a professor of special education at the University of Kansas, he directed numerous demonstration programs for students with autism spectrum disorder (ASD) and other disabilities and coordinated a variety of federal grant programs related to students with ASD and other disabilities. He also worked as a teacher of students with disabilities, a psychologist, and an administrator of programs for students with autism. He is the former editor of the professional journal *Focus on Autism and Other Developmental Disabilities* (published by PRO-ED) and the author of numerous books and articles on ASD.

Kevin M. Ayres, PhD, BCBA-D, is a professor of special education at the University of Georgia (UGA) and codirector of the Center for Autism and Behavioral Education Research at UGA. Dr. Ayres has worked in the field of autism and disability as a classroom teacher, a researcher, and a university instructor. His work has focused on behavior analytic applications of technology to meet the needs of individuals with autism and intellectual disability.

Erinn Whiteside, MAT, BCBA, is a doctoral student pursuing a PhD in special education at UGA. Ms. Whiteside has served as a supervisor for university-run model classrooms serving students with autism and other developmental disabilities, where multiple technologies are evaluated and implemented through evidence-based practices.